**Finding Personal Meaning and
Significance Through Landscapes**

TERRA SIGNS

Finding Personal Meaning and Significance Through Landscapes

Shana Robinson

Foreword by Colleen Deatsman

FLORIDA, 2016

Published by EWH Press
www.ewhpress.com

Copyright © 2014 by Shana Robinson
Terra Signs
Finding Personal Meaning and Significance Through Landscapes

All rights reserved. Except as permitted under U.S. Copyright Act of 1976, no part of this publication may be reproduced, distributed, or transmitted in any form or by any means, or stored in a database or retrieval system, without the prior written permission of the publisher.

ISBN 978-0-9903500-3-3
EWH Press first printing, December 2014

Cover and book design by Terrie MacNicol
Edited by Jeff Stoner

Printed in the United States of America

sign – n., an expression of meaning or sense placed within a pattern of significance

Dedication

To all those who nurture, especially Dana & the Roo...

Table of Contents

Foreword xi
Author's Preface xvii
Acknowldegments xix
Introduction xxi

Orient & Navigate: Thoughts About *Your* Land
    Exercise #1: Autochthony
    Exercise #2: Biophilia
    Exercise #3: Comparing Connection & Love

Chapter One: All Our Relations 1

Orient & Navigate: All Our Relations
    Exercise #1: Cosmogony
    Exercise #2: Space
    Exercise #3: Place

Chapter Two: The Shaman & Divination 13

Orient & Navigate: The Shaman & Divination
    Exercise #1: Personal Divination History
    Exercise #2: Beyond Divinatory Method into Awareness
    Exercise #3: Personal Omen Text

Chapter Three: Myth, Morality & Ethics 27

Orient & Navigate: Myth, Morality & Ethics
    Exercise #1: Toponyms & Tales, Apache-style
    Exercise #2: Toponyms & Tales, Penan-style

Chapter Four: The Metaphoric & the Metachoric 43

Orient & Navigate: The Metaphoric & the Metachoric
    Exercise #1: Personal Variations in Consciousness
    Exercise #2: Sonic Drivers
    Exercise #3: Mood Music

Chapter Five: What is a Landscape? 55

Orient & Navigate: What is a Landscape?
    Exercise #1: Describing
    Exercise #2: Mapping
    Exercise #3: The Language of Sensing
    Exercise #4: Heart Sensing

Chapter Six: The Work of the Shaman: Journeying & Divination ... 67

Orient & Navigate: The Work of the Shaman: Journeying & Divination
    Exercise #1: Clouds
    Exercise #2: Walking the Compass
    Exercise #3: Sitting Observations
    Exercise #4: Sensing the Story

Chapter Seven: Into the Picture 97

Orient & Navigate: Into the Picture
    Exercise #1: Contemplating Landscape
    Exercise #2: Alice's Looking Glass
    Exercise #3: Middle World Exploration
    Exercise #4: Connecting with a Maker
    Exercise #5: Visiting the Keeper of a Landscape
    Exercise #6: Visiting the Guardian of a Landscape
    Exercise #7: Landscape Art

Chapter Eight: The Terra Signs **111**

Freshwater 115	Mountains & Valleys 134
Forests and Woodlands 121	Coastline 140
Plains & Grasslands 126	Open Sea 144
Desert 130	Wild Earth 149

Orient & Navigate: The Terra Signs
    Exercise #1: Finding Your Seeds
    Exercise #2: Picture It

Chapter Nine: Those Who Dwell in the Land **161**

Orient & Navigate: Those Who Dwell in the Land
    Exercise #1: Who You Know
    Exercise #2: Favorite Tales
    Exercise #3: Cohabitants
    Exercise #4: Homes Under Threat
    Exercise #5: The Directions-Establishing Sacred Space

Afterword: Only the Tip of the Iceberg... .... **173**
    With or Without Walls

Appendix: Table of Cohabitants **177**

Endnotes **185**

Bibliography **197**

General Index **207**

Terra Sign Index **209**

Foreword

"I felt my lungs inflate with the onrush of scenery—air, mountains, trees, people. I thought, "This is what it is to be happy."
—Sylvia Plath, *The Bell Jar*

Forget not that the earth delights to feel your bare feet and the winds long to play with your hair.
—Khalil Gibran

These words from writers Sylvia Plath and Khalil Gibran speak of love. People love nature, and nature loves people.

It might appear that both writers are talking about two different things—the earth (nature, Terra) and people—each longing for the other and finding fulfillment in that connection. Yet, the earth and humans are not separate things; rather, they are one 'thing,' viewed through the eyes of a modern culture of duality.

We often refer to nature as a thing, or a place—something separate from us; however, that is a misnomer on several accounts. First, nature is not a thing; second, people are not things; and third, separation is an illusion.

Indeed, nature is not separate from us; we are one and the same. The very life force, elements, and energies swirling around us are also coursing through us. The same energy that causes the volcano to flow, the sprout to come to life in the spring and that signals the geese to fly south in the autumn, is the same life force that created, sustains and flows within everything—humans included. **We are** *nature*. In fact, there is an ancient universal law that speaks to this understanding: as above, so below; as within, so without.

Shamans understand that nature is the raw, untouched physical and energetic manifestation of life force energies and the interconnected, intertwining web of life. Nature is alive, dynamic and full of energies and forces that are both visible and invisible, known and unknown. Thus, nature is not a 'thing'; but rather, it is flowing movement that is alive with energy, essence, sentience, spirit and soul.

Similarly, we humans are not 'things.' We are energy—the same flowing energy that is nature; the same flowing energy that is soul; the same flowing energy we felt within us as carefree children and the same flowing energy that brings out the unburdened child in us from time to time. Children are naturals at connecting with nature and spirit because they love to explore, feel, sense, and experience all of life using all of their senses. Were you one of those children?

Did you love to go for walks, play ball with the neighbors, put rocks in your pocket, jump in puddles, climb trees, play for hours on the beach, wander off into cornfields, trek up a small creek or lay in the grass and gaze at the ever-changing skies? Do you recall that you could somehow 'see' without your 'eyes'—innately knowing how to sense, feel and experience things using your whole self? Well, this is exactly how shamans experience the world.

Do you long for those days again? Or did you perhaps miss out on those experiences and long for them now?

Because we are nature, we have a deep connection with nature—whether we are aware of it or not. Being in nature and contemplating nature deeply provides a much needed shift in perspective. Nature wears no mask. It is primal and direct. There are no dualities in nature—no good/bad, right/wrong, happy/sad, foolish/wise. There is only the soul of nature. By placing yourself in nature you can step aside from your duties and obligations for awhile and simply *be*.

What you find in that space may surprise you. It is said that when you lose yourself in nature, you find your Self.

Some people are mild observers, appreciating nature from afar, while others crave nature "up close and personal" and immerse themselves deeply in it whenever possible. Some dance in the middle. Whatever the means or the method, when we seek nature, we are also seeking our own essence. We long to feel the connection, raw energy and beauty of creation and destruction that nature provides…because it is also *us*. As artist Andy Goldsworthy says, "We often forget that we are nature. Nature is not something separate from us. So when we say that we have lost our connection to nature, we've lost our connection to ourselves."

The reality for most of us is that we live in a world that is fast-paced, ultra-busy, technological, and disconnected from nature. In some cases, people have become afraid of nature, separating themselves even further. No matter how slight—or extreme—separation from nature separates us from our soul essence, thus creating soul loss—a dangerous loss of the very essence of who and what we are at our core. Soul loss is a multi-faceted spiritual illness that can manifest physically, emotionally and mentally.

There was a time when we humans were not as separated from the natural world as we are today. We lived directly on the earth, in nature, a part of Terra—honoring the cycles of all things. As we have hidden our natural selves—and hidden *from* our natural selves—in the sterile boxes created for survival in the modern world, we have removed ourselves from the very energies that give us life. By abandoning the ways of living in harmony and balance with ourselves and everything around us, we have stepped away from life itself and have begun to destroy ourselves by destroying the very environment that supports us and all of life.

Thankfully, *Terra Signs*—the book you now hold in your hands—has arrived at this crucial and very critical time to help us fill a gaping hole in our lives, and in ourselves.

Terra Signs is a book about rebuilding balance and harmony. Through the very clear, concise and inspired work of author Shana Robinson, the reader is immersed in the 'what-is,' the 'why-do' and 'how-to' of what could be called "environmental shamanism." Shana does a brilliant job delineating for us exactly how the practice of shamanism can assist in reclaiming our connection with nature and with our own 'wild self.' By walking us through practices designed to connect us with the world of nature, spirit and soul, *Terra Signs* invites us to return to living on this beautiful planet from a place of reverence, enabling healing and evolution to a higher state of consciousness—both for ourselves and for Terra herself.

I appreciate that Shana teaches and writes from her own experience in sharing the special ways that she applies shamanic techniques and tools to forge a deep personal connection with Terra, our precious Mother Earth. There is a great deal of freedom working in this manner, as we are gently guided with ideas, suggestions and exercises, while being prompted to find our own way on the path. The guidelines, tools and techniques move us along while our own personal revelations keep our explorations fresh and inspired. As Shana takes us into the world of Terra and the work of the shaman, we can't help but see and directly experience how shamanism inherently connects us with our natural source and essence.

There are certain parts of nature that hold a special place in our hearts—we gravitate to these places; we are drawn. *Terra Signs* author Shana calls these places "sweet spots"—the special places that feed our souls. Perhaps it is a particular mountain, garden, forest, beach or park where you feel peace or excitement; calmness or joy. As you immerse yourself in these places you can feel the undiluted life force energies soaking into your bones. By deeply observing nature, by consciously being a part of Terra, and by journeying with the spirits of place through practices offered in *Terra Signs,* we find that we are doing more than connecting with nature, more than healing, more than following the footsteps of our ancestors. Perhaps for the first time, we find that we are actually gazing lovingly into the mirror of our very own soul.

Whether your journey is about finding yourself, healing, belonging to a place or wandering and exploring new places, it is a journey of opening to the raw energies of nature that stir your soul and awaken your inner fires of vitality. *Terra Signs* will help you connect with your "sweet spots"…and beyond. Prepare to be inspired!

"Come into the mountains, dear friend
Leave society and take no one with you
But your true self
Get close to nature
Your everyday games will be insignificant
Notice the clouds spontaneously forming patterns
And try to do that with your life."
—Susan Polis Schutz

Colleen Deatsman, author of *The Hollow Bone: A Field Guide to Shamanism* and *Seeing in the Dark: Claim Your Own Shamanic Power Now and in the Coming Age.*

Author's Preface

The tailings in the disused quarry reminded me of the foothills of Mordor, the land of the Lord of Barad-dûr. We had been trekking for most of the day, my job as camp counselor to keep the campers moving on our 25-mile hike from summer camp for an overnight at a friendly farm. Our feet crunched in graveled ruts—the only sound breaking the silence along this stretch of our journey. Trees were scarce and stunted, erupting carelessly from hillocks of jumbled soil and stone, defrocked of leaves in spite of the summer season. The grass was brown and thin as if the sun had leached most of the life out of it. Even the sky lent comment with a sullen gray splash of cloud that petulantly began spitting on our progress.

We trudged on. And on. Lunch of half-frozen meatloaf sandwiches and bug juice was ages ago. The promised stop for a water break was some point in the infinite future. Blisters began to shout in our boots. Nothing was the rose-color of our early and ambitious departure of the morning.

Suddenly we rounded a bend and stepped into an open field. As if passing over a threshold, noise returned to the typically boisterous crew, and a chorus of Granny's Lye Soap brought the usual good cheer accompanied by belches and farts from the boys. The air felt fresh and carried the fragrance of mown hay. Grasses swayed and heavy steps lightened. The clouds were swept aside with a breeze and we were released from the land of the Dark Lord.

Moments like this dance in and out of my memory when I think of times outside: summer camp, tenting with my family, hikes in the woods and hills. These experiences have initiated a quest for understanding and meaning from place and space. While my time in 'Mordor' was brief, it was filled with significance; places feel different and have a profound effect on us. How does this happen?

Acknowledgments

Books are tricky things. They often are the product of an insemination that takes years of incubation before their birth. Many moments and many beings—people and spirits—nourish the infant being until it finally is squeezed out into the world with trepidation and hope.

My gratitude begins with the land itself. Were it not for the many faces of Mother Earth, I would still be locked in sleep, not noticing the beauty and bounty that surrounds me. Her abundance bombarded me and I opened my eyes to see. She is the very root of my being and my sustenance—body, mind and spirit. And for her gifts of the Stone People, I give thanks. Since childhood I have collected and cherished stones and minerals, taking them with me on various wanderings at home and abroad.

Inspiration comes from stories like Mercedes Lackey's *Phoenix and Ashes*. Eleanor's travels into a set of Tarot cards as she learns her craft were the loom upon which *Terra Signs* was built. The warp and weft were song and poetry—"Ripplin' Waters," "Cold Nights in Canada," "Lines Composed a few miles above Tintern Abbey," "Sea Fever" and 'Regarding Wave," to name but a few.

My appreciation also extends to Michael Harner and the Foundation for Shamanic Studies. The practice of core shamanism is a blessing and a gift to our world.

For my Teacher and Allies, thank you! When ideas and directions seemed confusing, your persistent guidance was the spark that lighted the way.

If it were not for Jeff and Terrie at EWH Press, my dream of *Terra Signs* would be but a vague mist in my mind. They are the team that encouraged, prompted, niggled and nudged this book into being. Working with them is like working with an extension of myself, my family; they took *Terra Signs* beyond the limits of my vision and made the process a joy in creation.

More people than I can mention have shown me kindness, support and love, giving me cherished moments of heart-to-heart connection. You are the 'pearls on a string' that decorates my life. You know who you are! I bow to you in gratitude.

Thank you Mom for making me go to summer camp and Dad for my tree house. I love you!

And for my Dana. You listened to my talk of the 'landscape book' for over a decade and patiently supported the dream. Words cannot express my gratitude for your presence in my life and the gifts that you bring to me. Love you Monkin Man! You, too, Rocky Roo, for the walks you missed when mum was glued to the computer.

Introduction

Faced with uncertainty, humans over the ages have looked to the world around them for signs—signs to inform, affirm and guide. Although perhaps we are on better terms with our uncertainty than our ancestors, uncertainty persists and we continue to look for signs in our lives. Newspapers run astrology columns and cookies are baked with fortunes inside. Mediums contact the dead on television and divinatory card sets—tarot, medicine, animal, plant and angel—are sold in bookstores. We continue to look for direction from a guiding intelligence that tells us how to proceed and one that assures us all will be well.

A number of years ago I was riding with my husband Dana to Jamestown along the James River. We were going slowly, soaking in the scenery through a veil of light rain. As we eased our way down the road and through the marshland, I saw a wave of peace wash over his face. It struck me that he was in a landscape that had meaning for him; this was *his* land.

Pondering this, I was pulled back to a time when I was an expatriate in the United Kingdom. I traveled extensively through England and Wales, walking much of the countryside. After a day's hike over hill and dale, I'd sit in the bar of a small hotel sharing adventures and dreams of faraway places with fellow travelers. Inevitably we would conclude that each person had a special place, a landscape, where he or she was filled with excitement, vigor and belonging—a place where things felt 'right.' This sweet spot is where we find ourselves tied to the land in what Mircea Eliade calls autochthony. "It is the religious experience of autochthony; the feeling is that of *belonging to a place*, and it is a cosmically structured feeling that goes far beyond family or ancestral solidarity."[1] It is this connection to the land that is most often celebrated in indigenous cultures' birth, initiation and death ceremonies. It is reflected in the language of the *Rig Veda* ("Crawl to the Earth, thy mother") and Roman sepulchral inscriptions (*Hic natus hic situs est*, that is, Here was he born, here is he laid, and *Hic situs est patriae*, that is, Here he is laid in his native land).[2]

Places have an incredible sway over us. There is the man who wants to visit the 'old sod' before he dies and the high school senior who wants to 'go west' for college. It is in the trek to our ancestral past or the vista of our future that we often seek out landscapes to enrich the sense we have of ourselves. However, with the loss of landscapes through melting glaciers, deforestation, urban development, continued strip mining, and more, it has become critical that we gain an appreciation of the many faces Mother Earth wears before more are lost. Additionally, it is essential that we tap into the wisdom of these landscapes. Each one, from the short grass prairie to the ocean stack, has something to share that informs and empowers us. As the Siberian shaman's song goes, "All that exists lives."[3]

Landscapes surround us and are more than a backdrop to our activities. Whether or not we acknowledge them, their influence touches and colors our perceptions of the world. By actively acquainting ourselves with landscape through divination and journeywork, we open to the sea of wisdom and knowledge that surrounds us. And by doing so, we find those 'sweet spots'[4] upon the planet that fill us with wonder and nourish our spirit.

After each chapter of the book, a section called Orient & Navigate is included to establish a foundation for the ideas presented in the forgoing chapter. Rather than trying to respond to the Orient & Navigate exercises using only the limited space provided in the pages of this book, it is my suggestion that you photocopy each exercise and paste it in a journal specifically dedicated to this work. There are scissor icons in the exercises guiding you in cutting and pasting. Using the photocopy clips in your journal will give you more flexibility to fully express your thoughts—you have room to 'noodle and doodle.' To further eliminate limitations, I often use a sketching notebook as a journal; there are no lines on the page, and the paper is accepting of many media, from charcoal and colored pencils to felt markers and crayons.

Orient & Navigate: Thoughts About *Your* Land

Though we don't often think about it, we are tied to the land, be it the land we were born on or the land where we live. We are affected by places and landscapes. Just being on a mountain or sitting by a brook, feelings arise and our physiology responds.

✂ Exercise #1: Autochthony

autochthony – adj., nativeness, belonging to or being connected with a certain place or region

Consider this idea of belonging to the land. What place or places tug at you or suggest to you that you or a part of you belongs there? Make a list and see if you can pinpoint the nature of your connection to the place: born there, grew up there, work there, took vacations there, family cemetery is there, etc.

✂ Exercise #2: Biophilia

biophilia – n., love of life or living systems, living systems being landscapes and the life that plays out upon them

In his search for bliss, author Eric Weiner has applied this word to his experience of the Swiss Alps. In his engaging exploration *The Geography of Bliss*, he determines that happiness for the Swiss is boredom. He doesn't quite understand how they cope until he goes into the mountains and finds himself wrapped in a warm, fuzzy feeling and latches onto the word biophilia. Nature and natural places affect our physiology in ways we have yet to completely understand. Weiner concludes that the oxygen deficiency of altitude is not the basis for all nature-stimulated euphoria.[5]

As we begin the study of place and landscape, recall those places in which you may have experienced biophilia. For Dana, it was the marshland along the James River. One of my places is in the green rolling hills of upstate New York where a stream bounces from rock

Orient & Navigate: Thoughts About *Your* Land

to rock. You may have a number of places that sing to you and are sweet spots. As they come to mind, list them below. Ask yourself, What is it about these places that draws me or 'speaks to me'? Make some notes accordingly.

On the flip side are those places that give rise to fear or discomfort. If you feel so inclined, make a list of those.

Exercise #3: Comparing Connection (autochthony) & Love (biophilia)

Using the lists from Exercise #1 and Exercise #2, take a moment to compare them. What do you discover?

1 All Our Relations

My land is mine only because I came in spirit from that land, and so did my ancestors of the same land. My land is my foundation.
—James Galarrwuy Yunupingu, Chairperson of Northern Land Council[1]

My life's path propelled me into landscapes for answers and affiliation. I was an adopted child; my family moved around a lot. It wasn't easy to change schools and figure out the territory. I had fantasies of red-headed Celtic ancestors and aspirations for friends with a shelf-life of more than three years. As an observer of these musings, I see that I was always engaged in an ongoing search for belonging. Most of this energy lives in the past as part of a 'me' that once was. Today the quest is to locate myself in present time. Where is my sweet spot now?

I begin reviewing all the places I have lived, all the moves I have made, and I find a peculiar truth: I have made myself at home in any of a number of places against the backdrop of a multitude of landscapes, not always by choice but as a result of the vagaries of school, job and partner. I am struck with a profound realization: I am a nomad. Nomadism is a natural state of people seeking plant and animal sustenance, herders seeking pasturage. Yet for me, this is a strange and rather frightening realization. In my quest for belonging, nomadism seems to run counter to another of my basic instincts—to take root somewhere for community and survival. Nevertheless, here I am, driven perhaps through the coding instilled in me to move, seek and explore the whole of the Earth, not just one spot. I ease the panic that comes from this rootlessness with this consideration: I belong to the whole Earth. And, like the ugly duckling, I ask, "Are you my mother?" It is Mother Earth who answers, "Yes."

Panchamama.[2] Ina Maka.[3] Terra Mater.[4] Whether by indigenous people or by scholars, the Earth has been called 'Mother.' Like a human mother, our Earth Mother provides for our sustenance. Without Her, how would we eat? How would we breathe? To use Carl Sagan's description, Earth as seen from outside our solar system is a "pale blue dot" against the vastness of space.[5] Presently, we cannot leave the dot. Grasping the immensity of this insight, we understand our total dependence upon Mother Earth. We inextricably belong to Her.

Indigenous people who lived close to Nature have long recognized their connection to Mother Earth in various ways: sleeping on graves as a way to become a shaman; using soil from the graves of ancestors to connect with ancestral knowledge; chiefs marrying the land as a way to provide spiritual and secular leadership for their tribes; eating only foods from the soil upon which one lives to maintain optimum physical harmony. From the shamanic perspective, the Earth becomes the great She with a Spirit that manifests through many facets, landforms and life forms, with Keepers, Guardians and Makers who relate to us most intimately during our transitional periods—birth and death— on the physical level as well as through initiation on the spiritual level.

Connecting Newborns to the Earth

Humi positio is a Latin phrase that Mircea Eliade uses to convey the idea of 'giving birth on the ground.' It is a name applied to the ritual practice of laying a newborn infant on the ground to symbolize the connection between the child's physical mother and the Earth Mother she represents. This ritual is performed as a way to welcome a child into a community.[6] In parts of West Africa, a child is not considered fully born into this world until it has survived eight days. For the first seven days of its tenuous life, it is kept indoors; it is uncertain if the spirit of the child will choose to stay on Earth.[7] On the eighth day, early in the morning, the mother takes the child outside for the first time and places it on the ground under the eaves of the house. This part of the naming and 'outdooring' ceremony declares to the land that the newborn has arrived, survived and become part of the land, a family and an even wider community network. Eliade has commented that this autochthony—belonging to a place—is more than an acknowledgement of immediate family and ancestry, and suggests that the connection made to the land is a lifeline for the child's entire life.[8] The child and the Earth form a unit, each intimately tied to the other. This is demonstrated profoundly in a pre-outdooring rite performed by the child's relatives, in which the child's umbilical cord is sprinkled with herbs and placed in a calabash that is then buried under a tree at the rear of the house.[9] The cord that once tied the infant to the mother is now 'tied' to the Mother (Earth) and the child truly belongs to the Earth.

Nahua infants of Mexico gain protection from the Earth through a similar ritual performed by their fathers. When the umbilical falls from an infant, it is taken into the forest by the father and installed in the bark of a tree. In time it will grow into a pine tree, and the tree's kinship with the grown child will help the child conquer its fear of the night.[10]

Religions of the Book likewise recognize an uncontestable connection to earth (soil), if not *the* Earth (Mother, planet), as progenitor.

The Lord God formed man out of the dust of the ground (my emphasis) and breathed into his nostrils the breath of life, and man became a living being. (King James, Genesis 2:7)

Burial in the Earth: Initiation, Regeneration, Rebirth

Similar to the naming and outdooring ceremonies is the initiation ceremony. Whether it is a puberty initiation, a secret society initiation or a shamanic initiation, one premise is common to all: the initiand is becoming another, changing into something other than what he is in the present. Often, burial is used to symbolize a death to the old and a transformation into the new. In the Congo, boys are buried in the fetish house as part of their transformation into new men.[11] This notion of rebirth through earth has been extrapolated to include a kind of spiritual regeneration. Scandinavians believed that a witch's soul could be saved from eternal damnation if she were buried alive and a crop were sown above her grave and subsequently harvested.[12] The idea here, consistent with the burial of the boys in the Congo, is that whatever part rises up from the earth after the burial has been born through the Mother and thus renewed and cleansed.

Even today we feel the tug of the Earth Mother in times of change and challenge. I was in my first sweat lodge and needed all the help I could get. A group of friends and I had gone to the North Carolina mountains on a retreat to explore deeper levels of self and release old patterns; the sweat lodge was an integral part of the release.[13] It came time to enter the lodge and pray. As the hot stones were passed into the darkness of the lodge and participants pressed together in the mounting heat, my fears rose up in my belly. Before the drumming began, I was crying out my fears and felt that it was only the Earth who could give me solace. I remember shifting to my knees and pressing my head into the moist, cool ground. And there in the soil, I felt the heartbeat and embrace of Mother Earth consoling me. She held me through the ceremony until I emerged from the lodge, cleansed and reborn.

In many cultures, the living ones consider the dead who have been buried in the Earth to be ever present through their graves, able to convey power and knowledge. Though physically long gone, the ancestors can be accessed through their graves; it has been a worldwide practice to sleep on or lie near the graves of ancestors to receive their wisdom. The Euahlayi of Australia will take a novice to a cemetery and leave him there, bound, for several nights. During the course of his stay animals approach him, a man with a stick inserts a magical rock into him, and finally the spirits sing to him and teach him healing songs.[14] The Eskimos were also known to lie by graves to become medicine men.[15] Likewise, among certain North American tribal groups, individuals sought power by sleeping on graves. Closer to most of our Western ancestral roots are the practices of the Indo-Europeans. For the Celts in particular, prophets and poets became such by sleeping on the graves of relatives or ancestors.[16] In Faery Seership, a practice still very much alive in parts of the American South, it is recommended that anyone wishing to contact the ancestors keep upon one's altar a vial of soil, not only from the land upon which one lives, but also from ancestral graves.[17]

While the practice of sleeping on graves may have the ring of antiquity, it persists to this day. The Khakass, a group presently living in Southern Siberia, are situated in a landscape punctuated by graves. While they are not all shamans, the populace lives amongst gravestones that mark the pastoral landscape, organized along roads or next to villages. It is understood by the Khakass that the graveyards are the home to the ancestral spirits of one's own people, and thus represent a "good, light and comfortable place."[18] This awareness ties people to a homeland and forms the basis for a strong spiritual relationship to the land that has been threatened by industrial progress.[19]

There are some groups who are not so fortunate. The Buryat living in Mongolia have had to move from their traditional Siberian homeland under various political pressures. They have accommodated the resulting displacement and marginalization by developing a mobile history that connects them to their homeland. In ceremony, their shamans will call to the spirits, many of whom are ancestors, reciting the details of each—residences, places of birth and death—reminding the living of the lost homeland. When called into the shaman's paraphernalia—which is transported wherever the shaman goes—these spirits imbue the garments and tools with power and create a connection that sustains the link to the past and ancestral landscapes.[20]

Times of Sorrow and Death

Sorrow and death will also drive humans to the Earth. A friend recently lost his father-in-law, and the family created its own Earth ceremony to formalize the conclusion of his life. After he died, the man was cremated and the decision was made to return his ashes to the Earth. The family chose to do so at the bank of a river adjacent to a cemetery. This spot was important for two reasons: first, cemeteries and their surrounds are places usually undisturbed—with a sense of continuity; and second, the river was a place where the man's daughters used to play. Each family member took a handful of the man's ashes and returned it to the Earth while speaking what was in heart and mind. When all the ashes had been spread, the family washed their hands in the stream, completing the grieving process and symbolically shifting from mourning to cleansing and renewal. The river and its banks became a place of solace and connection for my friend and his family—a link through time and place where hearts, minds and bodies intersect with story and memory. Now, an ancestor is present in the landscape whenever they visit the river bank.

Marrying the Land

Prior to the influence of Christianity, the Celts had a tradition of *banais rigi*, or wedding of the kingship, that focused on the living Earth rather than the graves of the dead.[21] The leader or chief married the land. In Ireland, there was no central government or high kingship prior to the advent of Christianity. Instead there were smaller holdings called *tuaths*, each with a local chieftain. A significant linguistic marker for autochthony, the word *tuath* in Irish, has a combined meaning. Not only is it the dwelling land, it is also the people who live there.[22] By extension, the chief of the *tuath* is only granted sovereignty when he ceremonially marries the land which is his mother and, after the marriage, his wife.[23] This relationship with the land ensures that the chief will make the best possible decisions for his *tuath*—his land, as mother and bride, and his people. And it also implies that he will respect the *tuath* of another chief, since it would be the ultimate betrayal of his wife and mother to love another.

Eating Locally

The Eskimo people have a deep relationship with the wisdom of their landscape, especially the sea. In their songs they sing about the sea and the Spirit Woman beneath the waves. This Spirit Woman of the sea feeds them, satisfies their needs, and makes them happy.[24]

All humans are fed by their landscapes, although many people living in modern cultures today would find it difficult to say exactly how that's done. Some food has been so far removed from its original state that it is barely recognizable as plant or animal. There are, of course, different philosophies of eating and diet. One of these is macrobiotics, which claims that the ideal food to consume comes from the area where one lives. All things growing in a given region have had to learn to coexist and survive in a communal network of life. According to macrobiotic philosophy, the harmony found in the communal network is passed on to humans through consumption and leads to health.[25]

This same principle applies to the spiritual use of plants. Eliot Cowan, in his book *Plant Spirit Medicine,* shares the teaching of one of his mentors that plants growing locally have a thousand times more potency than non-locally grown plants when used as spirit medicine.[26] This speaks to the supporting harmony all beings share in a given locale.

Relationship to the Land

Looking at humankind's relationship to the land, the focus for many cultures has been one of kinship. The Earth is Mother, Wife and Provider. She has been respected as a living being in Her own right, a co-creator *with* humans. Her body reflects human activity as the business and busyness of humans impacts Her crust and mantle. She resonates and exchanges information with Her human partners and evolves along with them. In contrast, there are other cultures that view the Earth simply as an instrument to use for their own ends. This outlook strips the Earth of all spirit and makes the landscape a vast void—no information, no reflection, no exchange. The Earth is acted *upon*. When one ascribes to this outlook, there is an ever-increasing sense of alienation from the Earth, and the world becomes a hostile place, something to be conquered.

Daniel Stokols writes of these two ways in which to view the world—instrumental or spiritual. The instrumental view sees the environment as a tool and focuses on the material features. The spiritual view, on the other hand, emphasizes symbolic features of the environment and includes a richness of psychological and sociocultural meaning.[27] Stokols encourages us to examine our views of Nature and the Earth for the physical, mental and spiritual ramifications that result from holding them. As John A. Grim and Mary Evelyn Tucker point out, our Western Abrahamic traditions of Judaism, Christianity and Islam are anthropocentric, putting man ahead of all else, Nature is secondary.[28] This view has contributed significantly to what Eliade calls the desacralization of the Earth.[29] Humans no longer see the Earth as sacred, imbued with spirit. As a result, we become blinded to the signs in nature and become estranged from our Earth Mother, Wife and Provider.

Yet, deeply embedded in these same Abrahamic traditions, if we dare to look, are hints that Nature is sacred and a worthy partner. When Jesus became flesh and participated in Earthly life, he tacitly made all of Earth sacred. In Islam, the concept of *khalifa Allah* from the Qur'an makes humans vice-regents of Allah, suggesting that humans have a responsibility to Nature; that is, they must see and honor their relationship with it. And the covenantal tradition of Judaism creates a contract between humans and creation—a contract not unlike a marriage replete with duties and obligations.[30]

We live in a land of enchantment. We click on a computer or a television and the lure is set before us to *buy* something in order to *be* someone. In *The Sacred Santa* Dell DeChant discusses the myths of affluence we participate in via advertising.[31] Our attention is constantly drawn into the realm of material goods, and thoughts of the Divine or Creator are compartmentalized into a repetitious weekly service at best, or into a flurry of begging and bargaining in times of crisis. The Earth becomes the raw material to satisfy our avarice. Any contact with the 'supernatural' is eclipsed by the more powerful and surreptitious mandates to acquire, consume and dispose.[32] This cycle of consumerism is sustained by the de-spiritualization and objectification of the Earth. The instrumental view then overshadows the spiritual view, and the Earth is no longer an ally but rather a barren, sterile place without wisdom and heart—present only to sate our appetites. When this happens, humans find it easier to acquire better, more, bigger—but at what cost? This conflict is captured in a statement from Smohalla, a chief of the Wanapum, a Native American from what is now Washington State.

> *You ask me to plow the ground! Shall I take a knife and tear my mother's bosom? Then when I die she will not take me to her bosom to rest. You ask me to dig for stone! Shall I dig under her skin for her bones? Then when I die, I cannot enter her body to be born again. You ask me to cut the grass and make hay and sell it, and be rich like white men! But how dare I cut off my mother's hair?*[33]

What once was cooperation with the Earth as a conscious being has been replaced with a form of objectification that sets humans above the land and those spirits who inhabit it. This has led to loneliness and alienation. The purpose of this book is to support reconnection to the Earth as a spirited place with accessible intelligence and wisdom.

The next Orient & Navigate presents some vocabulary that will stimulate thinking about the instrumental and spiritual views of Earth. It is meant to get you thinking about the Earth as a stage upon which our souls play.

Orient & Navigate: All My Relations

It has been proposed that we each have a special or sweet spot on the Earth. In the words of Mircea Eliade:

"...to settle somewhere, to inhabit a space, is equivalent to repeating the cosmogony and hence to imitating the work of the gods, it follows that, for religious man, every existential decision to situate himself in space in fact constitutes a religious decision...he not only cosmicizes chaos but also sanctifies his little cosmos by making it like the world of the gods."[34]

Exercise #1: Cosmogony

Cosmogony - n., the order and pattern of the universe.

What is the cosmogony or universal pattern you are imitating?

Exercise #2: Space

Space – n., medium that holds action; an expanse in which all material objects are located and all events occur.

How do you make your space "the world of the gods?"

Orient & Navigate: All My Relations

✂ Exercise #3: Place

Place - n., a particular portion of space; the ground of human experiences, feeling and thought.

What can you do to settle into your place as if it were a decision based on a Divine calling, a deployment by Creator?

2 The Shaman and Divination

But we pedestrians – slow or fast – are far outnumbered by automobiles. Automobiles line the streets on both sides, parked nose to rump for as far as I can see on each and every street. They zip by at incredible speeds, their fat tires hissing…I learn quickly that I'm as good as invisible to the operators of these vehicles, and I cross the broad streets with the utmost caution.
—Peter in *The Watch* by Dennis Danvers[1]

The land has become as invisible as Peter, the pedestrian quoted above from Dennis Danvers' book *The Watch*.

Most towns, villages and cities in the past had a focal point and boundary markers. The village green, market square, well, wall, tower and moat informed residents and visitors of their place in space; they were cues people used to locate themselves.[2] You have to know where you are to relate to landscape. If there is a 'here,' then there is a 'there.' The contrast provides an appreciation for 'other,' which in the case of the city often becomes the countryside, a place where one encounters landscapes by virtue of an unimpeded vista.

However, urban sprawl is eliminating well-defined spaces punctuated by market squares and walls.[3] Sprawl has spawned suburbia—a vast homogenous space, dependent upon automobiles. The space has become 'nowhere' since it lacks uniqueness, and the people traveling in it become indistinguishable since they are so often isolated in cars. The problem with sameness is that the lack of contrast robs us of deeper, richer meaning. According to Mircea Eliade, the human experience of belonging and relating to the sacred is dependent upon heterogeneous perception.[4] For modern Westerners that requires a break in the monotony of strip malls, automobiles and sprawl. With the Earth being covered by the homogenous, we are in turn losing the sacred.

To grasp this alienation in another way, watch *Playtime,* a French film by the sensitive and comic Jacques Tati. His signature character Monsieur Hulot wanders through a modern French cityscape where uniformity and sterility extends from the architecture to the inhabitants. Even travel posters touting the fanciful colors of foreign locales are homogeneous; every destination highlights the same modern edifice. Tati conveys the sense that every 'nowhere' is the same.

Another observation from the character Peter in Dennis Danvers' book *The Watch* is illuminating: "I stop and stare [through a window]…It's television. An enormous automobile is rumbling up a beautiful mountainside to no apparent purpose except to demonstrate the sheer power of the thing, spewing rocks and gravel in all directions, bouncing over boulders. The geographer in me is horrified. Is there no concern of avalanche or erosion? What havoc might these behemoths wreak on a watershed?"[5] This reminds us of the words of Smohalla, from the last chapter, crying out against tearing into his mother's bosom. Peter's is a modern plea for a spiritual rather than an instrumental view of the Earth, one we must heed if we are to regain contact with the sacred. Humans may have big machines, but they are alienated from their world through acts that objectify it.

The Shaman

Exploring the world of the shaman can help us to regain our orientation in the world. By adopting a shamanic way of looking at and engaging everything around us, we can consciously create the break in homogeny that Eliade cites above as necessary for belonging and relating to the sacred. But who is the shaman? How does the shaman see the world?

The birth of the first shaman and the practice of shamanism predate the written word and may actually be preverbal. Yet, someone at some time in the past was able to slip between the cracks of this mundane, physical world and connect to other worlds and other beings. Finding help for everyday challenges in these worlds, she shared the fruits of the experience, and a tradition of contact with the spirits arose. Some made the transition to the other worlds with the help of the plant kingdom, using psychotropic preparations. Others flew to distant realms using the beat of the drum.

Anthropology, folklore and religious studies provide us with ethnographic records of shamans who, through divine election, inheritance, serious personal illness, or desire, were guided to assume the role of healer within their communities. While much work emphasizes the shaman as a healer, the shaman is also known as an adventurer, warrior and teacher.[6] We can use the methods of the shaman on our own quest to seek wisdom in the unseen worlds inhabited by spirits in order to rediscover the sacred and reconnect with the wisdom of the Earth.

The shaman is a person who *knows*. But what is it that is known? Through experience in traveling the realms beyond ordinary reality, the shaman knows that there are spirits, some of whom can become helpers or allies. The shaman knows the territories that the spirits inhabit and how to access them. The shaman knows the territory of death.

Perceptions of this mysterious figure—sometimes feared and often persecuted—have changed over the centuries. Many modern Westerners tend to think of shamanism as people 'acting like Indians.' While Native Americans and First Nations people have historically employed shamanism, the practice and accompanying techniques go beyond the shores of North America and are found world-wide. The word used to signify the body of knowledge comes from the writings of an exiled Russian Orthodox priest who encountered such a practitioner among the Siberian Evenki or Tungus people. In 1661, Avvakum wrote about a *saman* who called demons,[7] initiating a fear-based perspective that has slowly shifted over the intervening centuries to the point where scientists dialogue with shamans to exchange knowledge and world-views for mutual benefit.[8]

Popular interest in shamanism was stimulated about the same time that interest in Eastern meditation techniques became fashionable in the US—the 70s. In the surge of consciousness studies, researchers like Carlos Castañeda and Michael Harner contributed to a growing body of knowledge. While Castañeda's adventures, outlined in books like *Don Juan: A Yaqui Way of Knowledge* and *A Separate Reality,* portrayed an initiation out of reach for most people, Harner's work, presented in *The Way of the Shaman,* made the world of the shaman accessible. Castañeda introduced vocabulary to discuss shamanic experiences: ordinary reality is waking, objective, consensus reality; non-ordinary reality is what we experience on a shamanic journey while in an altered state of consciousness.[9] Harner condensed the techniques of the shaman to the basics that are evident in shamanic cultures world-wide and called the body of techniques 'core shamanism.' Core shamanism provides techniques to access the realms of the spirits; spiritual seekers explore without the cultural overlay of specific traditions.

There are many healers who work on behalf of their communities. Debate has flourished as to how to distinguish who is a shaman and who is not. Mircea Eliade, a religionist and teacher, has contributed to the definition we historically have used to make this determination. In his exhaustive work *Shamanism, Archaic Techniques of Ecstasy,* he makes it clear that it is the *ecstasy* that makes a shaman. There will be further discussion of this in a later chapter. *Ecstasy,* as it is called by Eliade, is the shamanic journey, the voyage of one's awareness out of his or her physical being to the other realms. Eliade is very clear in his work that this travel requires concentration; the final goal of the ecstasy is the soul's journey through the various cosmic regions.[10] The regions he delineates from his extensive, cross-cultural ethnographic study are sky, earth and underworld, which we have come to know as the Upper, Middle and Lower Worlds.[11] These worlds are connected by the Cosmic Tree, which is the *axis mundi,* or Axis of the World. The shaman customarily ascends or descends the tree to the other realms to do his work with the spirits.

Monotonous percussion is one of the methods the shaman uses to facilitate the shamanic journey or *ecstasy.* Studies have been conducted that give scientific weight to percussive stimuli as a consciousness altering technique used pervasively in ceremony and ritual.[12] Felicitas Goodman, among others, has called rhythmic stimulation a 'driving behavior' and hence we call the drum a sonic driver.[13] In Harner's work, the drum is used to trigger an altered state of consciousness (ASC) which he calls the shamanic state of consciousness (SSC).[14] In this state, one's body is relaxed and the mind is alert. It is in this state that we take a shamanic journey to meet helping spirits in the other worlds.

For the shaman, the physical world is one part of the universe, the other parts being the Lower and Upper Worlds—all connected by the great World Tree. Landscapes are important in the ordinary reality aspect of the Middle World, for they provide food, clothing and shelter to the shaman and her people; but in addition, landscapes in the other worlds of non-ordinary reality form the stages upon which spiritual allies live and communicate with the shaman. And more than that, the land in all worlds is a defining intelligence that in-forms the shaman and all creatures great and small, seen and unseen. For the Australian Aborigines, for example, the spirits themselves formed the landscape through their walks on the Earth's surface and their return through the Earth to the Dreamtime.[15]

Not only does the shaman speak to Nature—to the animals, plants, insects, fish, reptiles, rivers, mountains, clouds and sun— but the shaman also looks to Nature for signs, for communication originating in the natural world. Thus, Nature becomes a great informant for the shaman. In the early 1900s, for example, the Naskapi, a group of people living in Labrador, were observed to read sunbeams to locate lost or hidden objects.[16] From the shamanic perspective, any event out of the ordinary is potentially an important communication from Nature. It seems that as one works with the spirits of Nature and the other helping spirits found in the Three Worlds, one's own relationship with the land becomes deeper and deeper. In my own experience, I recall being in a visionary state and coming to understand, at the core of my being, that I was a particular representative of Earth and had come into being so that She could experience Herself through my personal perceptions.

The shaman stands between the physical world and the spiritual world as the two-way bridge between the people and the spirits. In this time of great change, as the power structure on the planet consumes more resources and more landscapes, it is the vision of the shaman that stands as a bulwark of sanity, ultimately of common sense: the shaman *knows* that our planet is precious and that its resources and landscapes are precious; the shaman *knows* that hidden within the natural world are great and wise spirits who can provide us with guidance as we face mounting problems and pressures. Ultimately, the shaman is a focus of hope in an increasingly chaotic and hopeless world because the shaman has not been blinded by the enchantments of the material world and still recognizes the Earth as a living partner.

Divination

Divination is one of the main tools of the shaman. In practice, it is the retrieval of hidden knowledge for the purpose of assisting oneself or one's community. While the shaman's journey is the prominent and distinctive way a shaman seeks information—actually a form of divination—there are many other diverse forms that can reveal hidden knowledge.

The foundation upon which divination of all kinds operates is the truth that underlying all that we see, know and experience—and all that is, even if we don't have knowledge of it—is connected, is one. What we perceive as individual, encapsulated beingness is what some would call a relative truth that allows us to engage a world where we explore, develop and heal relationships and separation. As we evolve and practice greater states of awareness, this relative truth yields to the absolute truth that all is one.

Julian Jaynes in *The Origin of Consciousness in the Breakdown of the Bicameral Mind* distinguishes four types of divination that have been used to gain insight into the world.[17] The first category includes what has been called the omen or omen text. This type of divination is passive and involves using the past as a cause and effect guide to the future. One waits for the portent and then reads it according to the text (if recorded) or past experience (as extracted from memory). This kind of reading becomes an historical or retrospective reading, as it is based on a pattern that has been built on experience over time.

One of my personal experiences with omens occurred on a kayak trip that lasted well into the night and was fraught with fears of having taken a wrong turn, missing the pull out, and being locked overnight in a parking lot. During the trip I saw a number of herons flying overhead and standing at the water's edge. I am particularly fond of these birds, and seeing them is always cause for elation. Since I saw so many on this particular misadventure, when it finally ended well, my omen became, "if you see herons, then all will end well." In a similar vein, a friend of mine had a relative who won a lot of money gambling at the casinos in Las Vegas. On the ride to the casinos, this woman had seen several funeral processions. Since then, my friend and her relative have adopted the omen: "If you see a funeral procession, then you'll have good luck gambling." While my friend is not a shaman, having such an omen in her awareness awakens her attention to economic opportunity and good fortune whenever she sees such a procession.

There are more broad-based examples of 'if-then' omens that have held sway over many years, even centuries, of human history, both in individual cultures or across cultures. Some of these more broadly held omens are still observable today. Astrologers use the planets and stars to make up natal charts that formulate the 'then' of individual personality and tendencies. If one is born under the sign of Mars, then one will have a temper. Other examples are the Rosicrucian traditions of menology (omens according to month) and hemerology (omens according to hour of day).[18] If one conducts a particular endeavor during a particular month or hour, the result will be either propitious or non-propitious, depending on the meaning assigned to the time. For example, a person in Period Two (that is, day 52 to day 104 after his or her birthday), is ill advised to begin a new career or enter into a contract during that time. However, it is a good time to move to a new home. Another example of a culture-wide omen, based on facial features, is found in Chinese medicine. If a person has a round face with thick nose and lips, they are of an earth nature and will be practical, frugal, thick-skinned and business oriented. A high forehead and long narrow face indicates a fire nature and the person will be quick tempered, nervous, forward, extremely bright, creative and talented.[19] Finally, dreams have been considered omens in many cultures throughout recorded human history. For example, an ancient Assyrian dream book said that if one dreamed of losing one's cylinder seal it meant that one's son would die.[20]

Another category of divination is sortilege, often referred to as the casting of lots. This is a more active form of divination in which a person asks a particular question and uses the selection of a marker to determine an answer. Choosing a rune stone from a pouch for guidance is a form of sortilege. Picking up yarrow sticks to determine which lines of the *I Ching* are applicable in a given situation is another example of sortilege. The answer and guidance comes from a limited set of possibilities. Dowsing falls into this category, since the answers indicated by the reaction of dowsing instruments—whether a pendulum, spring rod or angle rods—are limited to "yes-no-maybe-uncertain." To gain further insights, more questions are posed or another type of divination is used.

In the case of augury, a third category of divination, the reading of the answer is not limited by a set of possible interpretations. One gets more than an answer to a question; one gets hidden shades of meaning based on one's own interaction with the medium providing the answer. Any of a number of '-mancies' fit into this category. One of my favorites is myomancy. This is divination based on the movements of mice demonstrated by the mouse oracle or *gbekre* of the Baule of the Ivory Coast.[21] A special two chambered pot is used and the chambers are connected by a hole. A mouse is placed in the lower chamber and sticks covered with flour are placed in the upper chamber. A question is asked and the mouse, seeking the flour, crawls into the top chamber through the connecting hole and disrupts the sticks. The diviner looks at the patterns made by the sticks and uses them to provide a response to a question.

In augury, the idea of absolute truth—all is one—opens and clarifies. Fundamental to its operation, augury relies on the Hermetic Principle of Correspondence. This principle, which operates more subtly in omens and sortilege, states: "As above, so below; as below, so above."[22] The principle expresses 'all is one' while illuminating the number of planes of existence that are connected in relative truth. These planes range through matter, ethereal substance and energy,[23] as well as through mineral, elemental, plant, animal and human mental planes.[24] More to the point, and more easily comprehended in action are the Laws of Magic that apply. Isaac Bonewits in his book *Real Magic* highlights the law as the Law of Association which breaks down into the Law of Similars and the Law of Contagion. It is through association—a recognized set of connecting patterns—that objects and situations are entangled. This is reminiscent of quantum entanglement. "Although the two electrons may be separated by light-years, there is still an invisible Shrödinger wave connecting both of them, like an umbilical cord. If something happens to one electron, then something of that information is immediately transmitted to the other. This is called 'quantum entanglement,' the concept that particles vibrating in coherence have some kind of deep connection linking them together."[25]

Coherence in magical laws operates through similars and contagion. With similars, one object is identified with another. As Bonewits notes, "Look-alikes are alike."[26] With contagion, things that have been in contact with one another continue to interact even after separation. Regarding contagion, Bonewits comments, "Power is contagious."[27]

Augury uses a medium that is personally interpreted. This medium may be smoke (capnomancy), hot wax in water (ceromancy) or oil on water (leconomancy), for instance. All of these activities are metaphorical in nature, deriving meaning from the Law of Association. For example, one of the most widely used auguries is scapulomancy, the reading of animal shoulder blades. For the Naskapi of Labrador, it was the message of the scapula that provided a key to survival when they faced the constant threats of freezing, starving and drowning at the turn of the last century. The shoulder bone of a bear, beaver or hare was exposed to fire or hot ash and then read. The resulting cracks and spots on the bone were indicators of future events or the best possible path for a journey.[28] Applying the Law of Similars, the bone 'becomes' the snowy terrain of the journey and the cracks 'become' the track showing the way. Another applicable law in augury is the Law of Contagion. To find out about the prospects of a fishing trip, for example, the Naskapi would toss the jawbone of a fish into the air, *icthyosteomancy* (reading fish bones—my word). The way it landed gave them an indication as to the success of a fishing trip.[29] Because the jawbone came from the same species of fish sought on the fishing trip, the 'contagion' provided the connection through which normally unknowable information flowed.

Jaynes' last category of divination is spontaneous divination. It is free from a specific medium, opening the interpretive field to everything, and is also highly metaphorical in nature. In this case, a question is posed and then the questioner looks out into the world to see what stands out. When attention is drawn to an object, the object is then read to see what message can be gleaned. This kind of divination has been used throughout the ages and takes 'all is one' to an even deeper level. In this, the querent is acutely mindful of the personal entanglement with all that he encounters.

These divination categories involving texts, coins, and various other objects can be grouped together and considered inductive divination—that is, divination based on observations. The final category of divination in this scheme is ecstatic divination and includes the shamanic journey. Ecstatic divination occurs when one gets information directly from the spirits. Using the journey, the querent goes to the spirits for an answer. However, in culturally specific situations, as in the case of Mongolian shamans for example, rather than travel to the spirits via the journey, the shaman calls the spirits to her and they will speak through her. The shaman as medium or channel is engaged in ecstatic divination, acquiring information directly from the spirits. This activity has been influential in expanding the definition of *shaman*, which will be discussed further in Chapter 6.

The shaman's worldview and the practice of divination are ways of deeply perceiving the world and our place in it. Using the skills of the shaman, modern humans can reconnect to the sacred and gain information for personal or communal benefit. Once this connection is reestablished and we acknowledge our entanglement with all that is, the signs coded in landscape become accessible.

Through the next Orient & Navigate we can begin to appreciate the ways that our world already informs us. Whether we are simply curious or whether we are heavily invested in acquiring information, there are ways that we interpret or divine events in our lives and make decisions using divinatory forms. Some we may engage playfully; others we may take very seriously.

Orient & Navigate: The Shaman & Divination

Exercise #1: Personal Divination History

What kinds of divination have you personally used to answer questions?

Using Jaynes' categories, what have you consulted?

Omens? (What is your astrological sign?)

Sortilege? (Have you ever tossed a coin?)

Augury? (Have you ever felt unsettled upon pulling the Ace of Spades from a deck of cards? Why? What other associations have you made that yield meaning for you?)

Spontaneous? (Have you encountered something unusual on a walk and felt that it held meaning for you, perhaps how the rest of your day would proceed?)

Orient & Navigate: The Shaman & Divination

✂ **Exercise #2: Beyond Divinatory Method & into Awareness**

What's the most recent event in which you recall some kind of knowledge coming to you that had meaning and informed you?

✂ **Exercise #3: Personal Omen Text**

Do you have a personal omen like the heron or funeral procession story? (Perhaps there is a song or particular artist that airs on the radio or Muzak® whenever you are in a certain situation?) Share your omen story here.

3 Myth, Morality & Ethics

After every foolish day we sleep off the fumes and furies of its hours; and though we are always engaged with particulars, and often enslaved to them, we bring with us to every experiment the innate universal laws. These, while they exist in the mind as ideas, stand around us in nature forever embodied, a present sanity to expose and cure the insanity of men.
—Ralph Waldo Emerson, "Nature," from *Essays*[1]

It is night and we have gathered around the campfire. The crackle of the flames drives away the chill and we pull closer together to bathe in the golden light. The world around us is overtly quieting. Dogs turn in circles to settle; the chirping of the birds is hushed; the droning of the bees has stopped. Yet, deeper in the night, things are stirring. The nighthawk whooshes by on his errands. Chuck Will's Widow sings out her name. Owl wings brush the air and a rabbit squeals. Minds and hearts move in response to the great questions of existence. Looking up at the stars, we wonder: where did all creation come from? Why am I here?

Humankind's big and little questions about where we came from and how we should live have often been answered through story. Joseph Campbell examines these stories or myths and explains that we've lost respect for them in this current age. We don't see them as truthful and erroneously relegate them to an inferior status. He wisely corrects us and says that myths operate on a different level of truth and are just as potent as our scientific explanations. In fact, Campbell says that the "whole secret relating mythology to spiritual life [relates] to your environment."[2] Myths inform us about ourselves and our relationship to the world in a much richer way than the cold data of science. This is not to say that science is unimportant, but it is to recognize that each form of truth has its place in a balanced, healthy society.

When we look at place, therefore, we are looking not at a barren physical space, but rather, as Gregory Cajete points out, a place that has soul and a natural orientation.[3] This means that there is intelligence and meaning locked into place that can be sacred, as when a place represents a universal power such as a deity—or it can be *loric*, as when it represents a more local or unique power. Walter Brenneman talks about this difference when he relates his experience of entering groves near wells in Ireland. The groves were places that encompassed and drew him inward and were places of intimacy unto themselves, versus other places where a sense of expansion prevailed. He chose to use the term *loric* in defining such places because like lore, they depended upon the individual response to them for their power in the way a story depends on the artistry of a particular storyteller; the groves are experience-specific locations dependent upon the individual at the moment of meeting.[4]

This sense of experience-specificity Brenneman discusses has its roots in the Irish tradition of place lore called *dindseanchas*. The *dindseanchas* are place name stories and are among the earliest tales that come from Ireland. There are three collections of these stories: The Metrical Dindshenchas, the Banshenchas and the Prose Dindshenchas, all of which draw from the Book of Leinster compiled about 1160.[5] Ireland itself was seen as a living goddess, and each and every feature from hill to stream was a living story of an associated spirit—either a deity or an ancestor. To hear the word 'Tara,' for example, was to know through stories of the history of this central 'hill' from which the kings of Ireland ruled. It became 'Tara' when the name changed for the fifth time, honoring Te'a, the wife of Eremon, an invading chieftain.[6] Uisnech, another hill, captures a story in name by referring to the way a young man protected the first fire of Erinn from the Druids. Midhe, the young man, and his clan were responsible for maintaining this fire from which all other fires were lit and for which the clan received payment from every household. When a Druid plot to undermine this exchange was uncovered, Midhe attacked the Druids and cut out their tongues. He buried the tongues on the hill and his mother exclaimed that "he proudly sat" (*uaisnech*) on the hill, from which Uisnech as a place name is derived.[7] The name of the province Meath comes from Midhe. Knowing the names of these places not only tells us which ones and where they are, but also provides a history of place and underscores its importance.

In Iceland there is also a tradition of land-taking and naming. It is called *landnám* and is recorded in Landnámabók, the book of settlement. In this strange book, land is claimed through the naming of the landscape and the names can be used to trace families and their important events. These links joining families to places are not dry historical references. Underlying this is a tradition that recognizes spirits in the landscape, very powerful forces that are still active today. According to a *New York Times* article, many Icelanders believe in nature spirits, elves specifically, that live in the rocks of the harsh terrain. People will go to great lengths to avoid disturbing such rocks, especially those reputed to be elf habitats.[8]

Recognizing who or what lives in and on the land was an important practice for the Taoists in China as well. As some of the earliest practitioners of *feng shui*, the Taoist priests were asked to advise on the placement of graves in order to avoid the bad luck that would be visited upon relatives by wrathful ancestors.[9] The art of grave placement evolved over many years and is still practiced today to create harmonious spaces for the living through *feng shui*. *Feng shui* is concerned with *chi* and form.[10] *Chi* is life force and it flows in the earth, the atmosphere and our bodies. Form relates to shapes such as hills or swamps. The life force flows through all forms and can contribute to health and a state of well-being, depending on the flow. Placement on the forms is done with *yi*—that is, intention—to work with the special powers of the landforms—powers of dragons, tigers, snakes, elephants and phoenixes, for example. Master Lin Yun, the renowned expert on *feng shui* from the Black Sect of Tantric Buddhism, shared with author James Swan that his home in Berkeley sat on top of the head of a dragon whose tail extended down the street to the water of San Francisco Bay. He explained that this placement on the dragon's head helps the *chi* rise upward and aids his spiritual connection.[11]

The Japanese have a similar worldview that comes from Shinto mythology. The *kami* (spirits or gods) live in everything from rocks and trees to hills, caves, oceans and mountains.[12] Mountains play a particularly important role in shaping the living environments of the Japanese, so much so that Tadahiko Higuchi categorized seven types of mountainous configurations for the building of shrines and temple complexes.[13] Parallels can be seen between his list and the most auspicious *feng shui* placement: on a rise at the head of a valley with tapering ridges creating a sense of enclosure without restricting views. For the Chinese, being on a rise encouraged dragon energy to flow down to the dwelling and its inhabitants; and if water was to the west, it provided a barrier to unpredictable tiger energy.

Similar to this notion of indwelling spirit is the Khanty idea of soul or *lil'*.[14] The Khanty, a Western Siberian group, bring meaning to landscape features through the recognition of *lil'*. When a feature in the landscape resembles a human or an animal, it is thought to be *lilenky* or animate. Also, should a *lung* (a supernatural being) inhabit a stone or tree stump, it too becomes animate.[15]

The Khanty are hunters and to ensure a good seasonal hunt, they make gifts to *Wuhnt Lung*, the forest spirit. The gifts are taken into the boggy terrain of the taiga and left on the *kot mykh* or earth houses. These earth houses are the residence of *Wuhnt Lung* and are easily recognized as isolated islands rising up from the open bog.[16]

Much of what these examples from other cultures signifies for us is that, consciously recognized or not, place has meaning. Whether we climb the highest mountain or enter into the darkness of a cave, the natural world speaks to us. The meaning or significance can come to us through toponym, that is place name, which can be a story in itself (like Brenneman's loric perception), or it can come to us as part of a grander etiological tale of creation and the gods. It can even come to us in the form of a 'just so' story, where the mysteries of the natural world are explained in ways to make a point, explain something or to make us smile. The stories themselves have purpose, too. Place names tie events to specific locales, and places become record keepers, a mnemonic of landform that keeps a group's history and life lessons alive.

An interesting example of this comes from Borneo. The Penan are a people living on the island, and their landscape is mountainous, extensively covered by tropical forests and carved by many large rivers.[17] The Western Penan are hunters and gatherers, living in the interior of Borneo in the Belaga District and in the Silat River watershed.[18] For these people, the most important features of their landscape are rivers and streams. Due to their reliance on rivers, rivers become the reference points for all other aspects of landscape.[19] It is an intimate understanding of rivers and the way they flow that allows the Penan to navigate through their forests using the riparian topography as guidance. The relationship to rivers runs so deep that the Penan, according to J. Peter Brosius, will frequently speak of their territories as "the rivers from which we eat."[20] Landscape informs the Penan through the toponym. One river is named Be Laké Kulit Pelu ∃it. In the 1950s a man named Laké Kulit died while passing by. He was resting near a steep slope and after falling asleep, fell down the slope and was killed. Pelu ∃it is the word for tumble. Thus, the river became known as the place where Laké Kulit tumbled down.[21]

Interestingly, there is also a practice among the Penan of refraining from naming the deceased. So rather than using a deceased individual's name, the place where the death occurred or where the person is buried is used.[22] And since the referent for these people is a river, the name of the river and the watershed becomes the signifier for the deceased or his burial place. In this way, knowing place names and the human connections to them maintains the knowledge of family history and genealogy for the Penan. When rivers and forests are threatened by logging, it is Penan biography that is threatened.[23] Their landscape isn't sacred in the sense of connection to an overarching deity as in a Westerner's view of the sacred, but rather it is imbued with cultural significance that is deeply connected to their sense of identity and history.[24]

The Western Apache likewise look to places and their names not for biography or history, as do the Penan, but rather for wisdom. To the Apache, wisdom is a capacity that is developed to keep one safe through the avoidance of mishaps. To develop wisdom one must develop a smooth, steady and resilient mind that can see things before they happen.[25] This can be accomplished through the attention to and assimilation of various lessons tied to places and recalled via the toponym. At its simplest, a child may be told a story about a place that becomes an object lesson. Keith Basso, who has researched the wisdom of Apache places and place names, relates one such story as told to him by his informant Ruth.

When Ruth was a young girl she was digging mescal with her family for roasting. She was not strong and easily became tired. Her mother admonished her to not be lazy and to not think about being tired. She told her daughter that if she thought about being tired she could get hurt. Ruth's mother went on to relay a tale about a young girl who was sent into the mountains called Whiteness Spreads Out Extending Down To Water to collect wood. Returning from her task she was tired and inattentive. She carelessly stepped on a thin rock and when it broke, she fell and was knocked unconscious for a while. Upon her revival, she returned to her camp, where her mother chastised her for not seeing the danger in the thin rock before stepping upon it. When she finished the tale, Ruth's mother told Ruth to remember that this happened at Whiteness Spreads Out Extending Down To Water, the place where a careless girl almost died. To this day, Ruth recalls this tale and tells it to all the children. It is a way she teaches them to pay attention while doing tiring work. The lesson is completely captured in the place name—the place name itself contains the lesson of caution—and fosters the kind of wisdom that can limit accidents. The beauty of tying the story, the lesson and the place name together is a form of embodiment in the landscape. Just looking at or speaking of Whiteness Spreads Out Extending Down To Water reinforces the story and the lesson.[26]

Used in its more complex form, naming places and knowing what happened in those places becomes a means for face-saving candid expression and reinforcement for moral behavior.[27] While riding with some Apache horsemen, Basso witnessed a conversation they had with a younger, troubled man. The discussion of horses ceased upon his approach and the young man who had been acting out over a failed relationship—drinking too much and propositioning other women—began to speak. He apologized to the men and told them he'd been sober for several days and that he was anxious to get away from the ridicule and gossip his behavior had unleashed. Rather than the empathetic response Basso expected, he heard a perplexing series of comments. "So! You've returned from Trail Goes Down Between Two Hills." "So! You got tired walking back and forth." "So! You smelled enough burning piss." The young man responded, "For a while I couldn't see." The conclusion from the horsemen: "Trail Goes Down Between Two Hills will make you wise. We'll work together tomorrow."[28]

To unlock the mystery of this exchange, one has to know the story of Trail Goes Down Between Two Hills. It is a very real place, with two wooded knolls, a path that passes between them and a big cottonwood tree. The ancestors told a story about events that transpired there. The tale involved Old Man Owl, who liked women and wanted to sexually engage them. When he was walking one day, two girls decided to tease him. They each climbed a knoll and proceeded to call him back and forth between the two with the promise of womanly charms. He never reached the top of either hill because as he neared it, he was called to the top of the other. He went back and forth four times and the girls laughed at him. Later, the same sisters again encountered Old Man Owl. One climbed the large cottonwood tree and exposed herself to him. Being of poor sight, Old Man Owl thought it was a sexy bit of tree he was seeing and decided to burn the tree down to take the attractive bit home with him. He lit a fire and the sister in the tree pissed on it to put it out. He wondered where the rain was coming from and lit another fire. Again the rain came and put the fire out. This happened four times before Old Man Owl gave up and went home, leaving the girls laughing.[29]

In the exchange between the horsemen and the youth several things are noteworthy. Because the horsemen and the youth were unrelated, none of the horsemen had the authority to comment on the young man's behavior. And, because the young man had come to them apologetically backing it up with three days of sobriety, any further criticism would have been harsh; the youth had already discovered his inappropriateness and taken steps to change. Therefore, the men conversed with him in the metaphor of the Trail Goes Down Between Two Hills story. Comparing the youth's past actions, and the youth himself, to Old Man Owl acknowledged that the young man's actions had been foolish but they were now behind him. Continuing to affirm the youth's change of heart, the horsemen reiterated the foolishness of Old Man Owl by reminding the boy of the burning piss and that the boy had had enough of it. The message was clear for those raised with the story; it is shortsighted to indulge in sexual appetites and it leads to discord. The young man then asserts that he has faced up to his misconduct and won't be revisiting it by saying "For a while [like Old Man Owl] I couldn't see."[30]

This brief communication between the horsemen and the young man contained a confession, a chastisement and a pardon ("We'll work together tomorrow"). Anyone who knows Trail Goes Down Between Two Hills and the story about it has access to the wisdom locked into that place and can use the place as a fixed reminder of the lesson. The story serves as moral guidance, and the young man can use the place and the story to develop a smooth, steady, resilient mind.

In a conversation with a traveling companion, Bruce Chatwin, author and traveler, asks of her, "You're saying that man 'makes' his territory by naming the 'things' in it?" She replies emphatically, "Yes, I am!"[31] The conversation took place in Australia, the land Down Under, where the enchantment of songlines and Dreamtime delights us and demonstrates yet another response to landscape's compelling power. From the Aborigines to the Colonists, the naming of place is essential to initiate attachment and caring. Kazuo Matsubayashi writes of his own experience of returning to the U. S. from a sabbatical in Japan. As he entered Salt Lake City, he felt like he was coming home. He concluded that to put down roots in an area is to develop an attachment to it; from this attachment, a spirit of the place arises and one cares.[32] For the Colonists in Australia, the subtle means of connection to place can be seen in the use of place names: Queenstown, Stonehenge, Northumbria Hill—all very British, harkening back to home. Other place names capture events: Misery Plateau, Desolation River, Lake Repulse—all evoking the common difficulties of life in a new land. These names were used to make the unfamiliar familiar in an effort to foster connection and caring.

During the same conversation with Chatwin, another observation was made: plants that did not grow in an Aborigine's territory had no name. Having no name actually had the deeper meaning of "doesn't grow in my country."[33] On the contrary, those things within the territory—upon which an Aborigine depended for life—had names, very specific names. The act of naming minerals, flora and fauna intimately tied the Aborigine to the land and ensured survival.

For the Aborigine, even deeper ties to the land are evidenced through the songlines. It is through the songlines that a kind of custodianship or ownership of a given territory is established and maintained through heredity and trading. In the beginning of things, the Ancients sang the world into life through naming. They called out "I AM" and what was named, be it snake, river or dune came into existence. These ancestors walked about the land singing it into being, decorating it with things, leaving trails of song and music in their tracks. These trails of music and song are the songlines, and the Aborigines each inherit a stretch of song and the land over which it passes from the ancestors.[34] In addition to the inherited connection to the songlines, a child alerts his mother to his personal place on the land at his first kick. It is at this moment, as his pregnant mother is moving about, that a spirit-child left by the Ancients travels up through the mother's body to the yet unborn child in her womb and gives it song. The mother informs the Elders of this quickening, and they in turn determine by the lay of the land which Ancient left which song and which stanzas will become the child's personal music to 'own' and care for.[35] Once again, the attachment to place through the song of the ancestors creates caring and identity.

Landforms also have associated stories, many of them etiological. Chatwin recorded a number of these while touring Australia, including one explaining why railway tracks traversed an additional two miles. The original track had been slated to cut through a particular hill. In seeing if that would be a problem, the 'owner' or Aborigine tending the song passing through the hill was sought. In the eleventh hour, a group of Aranda men showed up and cautioned the railway workers against cutting into the hill and releasing Maggot Power. The story-song was that an ancestor of the Dreamtime hadn't correctly performed a ritual that would control the breeding cycle of a bush-fly. Maggots overran the area and the ancestor was forced to stuff them under the rock of the hill where they had been breeding ever since. To cut into to the rock would release them and it would be the end of everything; they would explode into the world and kill everything with poison. Heeding this warning, the railway company adjusted its tracks.[36]

Another story was about the Lizard Man's resting place—another hill—where Lizard Man lay down to die after journeying to the south with his wife. On the journey he met a stranger who wanted his wife. In the course of events, the stranger swapped his ugly, disguised wife for Lizard Man's wife, thus deceiving Lizard Man. Lizard Man returned home with the substitute wife, died and became the hill. Lizard Man Hill was a place, a song and an inheritance of an Aborigine…and was also avoided by the railway company.[37]

Halfway around the world and perhaps more familiar to Westerners are the beautiful Dolomites. These limestone mountains are part of the Eastern Alps in Italy and are the subject of many lovely tales. One such tale tells of an earthly prince who longs to visit the Moon. He eventually does so and meets the princess of the Moon. They fall in love, but he soon discovers he cannot remain on the Moon or he'll go blind. They go to Earth together, but the princess is so homesick for the Moon she almost dies of longing. She returns to the Moon and the two are separated by their afflictions—his possible blindness, her homesickness. Along come the Salwans, dwarves displaced by invaders, looking for a new homeland and not meeting with much success. They meet the prince, who is languishing on Earth, and strike a bargain with him. They will make the mountains where he lives white like the Moon in exchange for a place to live. The prince agrees and the Salwans work their magic. Soon the mountains glow like the Moon and the prince and princess are reunited. The prince has his princess and she no longer is homesick for the Moon, because the Dolomites are more beautiful than the Moon. Today the prince and princess are long gone, but the Salwans remain and the homesickness of the princess still taints the atmosphere. Anyone who has visited the Dolomites is touched by it and will forever long to return to the Moon-like mountains.[38]

From these stories it can be seen that people across many cultures have been intimately connected to the land and landscape, as evidenced by toponyms and stories. Not all connections are 'sacred' in the Western sense that bespeaks numinous experience. Many connections are socio-cultural and serve as reminders of behavioral proscriptions, historic events and kinship. What is common is that for those born to the land and enculturated to it, there is wisdom inextricably bound to the land and its many forms—wisdom that is alive and demands a voice and the utmost respect.

The next Orient & Navigate encourages you to think about space and place in an intimate, personal way. Using the models of the Penan and the Apache, you will have the opportunity to consider the land in a way that isn't necessarily 'sacred,' but very important nevertheless.

Orient & Navigate: Myth, Morality & Ethics

Families often have stories that are shared as part of teaching youngsters.

Exercise #1: Toponyms & Tales Apache-style: Morals for a Strong, Resilient Mind

One of my favorite stories involves my father as a young boy. His mother's family, the Blakes, had property in the country. My father used to enjoy going to the farm and had been told repeatedly not to mess around in the barn. Boys being boys, he loved the barn and enjoyed the secrets of the hayloft. While horsing around one day, he leapt from the hayloft and, upon hitting the ground, so rattled his teeth that he almost bit his tongue off. My grandmother did what any strong farm woman would do when he came in crying. She sat him down, gave him some whiskey and proceeded to sew the hanging bit of tongue back onto the main muscle using needle and thread. Upon the retelling of this tale, my father would laugh and exaggerate the whiskey and needle. But the point he was making was that had he not been horsing around, he wouldn't have had to undergo Nana's rather primitive medical treatment.

This tale could be named as "Dad Jumps From the Hayloft" and reflect the nature of an Apache Tale. It has connection to a place—*the* hayloft on *the* farm—and it carries with it an admonition not to horse around in potentially dangerous places.

Take some time and think about your family stories, the ones that get repeated at family gatherings so often that even mentioning "the time that…" gets people laughing. Write the story and name it. See if you can connect it to a place. Extract the moral of the story. Does the story have more impact now that you've looked at it in this manner?

Orient & Navigate: Myth, Morality & Ethics

Your Story's Name:

Your Story:

Orient & Navigate: Myth, Morality & Ethics

Exercise #2: Toponyms & Tales, Penan-style: Family History

Like the Penan, families often have various places on the Earth that are associated with family history. These places are not sacred in the sense that contact with the Divine happened on the spot, but rather they are important because of the impact of the event. These are the places worthy of family trailside interpretive boards—your family's version of a sign that says, "George Washington slept here."

I have several such places that readily come to mind. One is the tree my young cousin Bobby crashed into after a football victory in which he was the star quarterback. The collision led to his death. If I were to mention Bobby's Tree to anyone along that branch of my family, they would immediately connect to the tragedy. Another example is Racquette Lake in upstate New York. Mention this to the right clan and hoots of laughter will rise up as everyone recalls the time my dad and my cousin went canoeing on the lake and had their packs torn apart by hungry bears.

What place names tell a story for you? Your family?

Place Name:
Associated Story:

Place Name:
Associated Story:

Place Name:
Associated Story:

4 The Metaphoric & the Metachoric

I am asked about the difference between visualization and a vision of the alternate reality. A visualized image is your own creation; a vision comes about when you see what is 'out there,' the alternate part of reality.
—Felicitas D. Goodman, *Where the Spirits Ride the Wind*[1]

Landscapes historically are enculturated—that is, they have meaning according to one's culture. However, in the modern Western world, individuals have their own ways of relating to a given landscape based on personal experiences and memories. Faith Popcorn partially captures this trend in what she calls cocooning.[2] Humans tend to pull back from a community at large and isolate themselves as a protective response to harshness and unpredictability. This promotes individual interpretations of the same experience. As we work with landscapes, we need to develop personal metaphoric systems. We will not adopt an established system or develop a consensus. This will be a process of discovery for each individual. Many of the interpretations will resemble each other. However, there will be shades of difference that make each individual's metaphor distinct and highly personal.

By way of explanation, here is how one element of landscape, a river, might be used by two individuals as a metaphor. For one, the flow of water in the river represents the flow of prosperity. When the flow is met with fear, there is a sense of contraction and lack. When the flow is met with certainty, there is adventure. The river and its flow become an opportunity to choose an approach to prosperity: fear or certainty. For another person, the river may represent personal development—the nature of the flow having to do with ease of progress and changes of circumstance. A strong flowing river represents a good, healthy direction while an eddy represents an unwanted detour or distraction in one's life course. While there is an underlying harmony between the two interpretations, each base is a slightly different metaphor, thus demonstrating the necessary individuality of interpretation.

The shaman engages landscapes in ordinary reality to access information and can do the same in non-ordinary reality. The landscapes of non-ordinary reality are encountered on the shamanic journey, the *ecstasy* discussed in Chapter 2. Each of the three cosmic zones—the Lower, Middle and Upper worlds—can be entered using specific techniques and are the territories in which the shaman encounters and establishes relationships with beings that inform and instruct.[3]

While our journey experiences can be described as *seeing* seeing is really a metaphor. We aren't seeing with our eyes or watching things unfold on the back of our eyelids. We perceive information with multiple senses, as if we are using our eyes, only it is without the benefit of an external physical stimulus. This has been called hallucinating or 'having visions.'

Typical vision requires light from an object to enter the eye and stimulate the retina. The stimulated retina sends signals to the brain as electro-chemical impulses that are then interpreted. In entoptic vision, the visual effect occurs within the eye itself without benefit of an external object and light entering the eye. Phosphenes, a kind of entoptic experience, occur when you see lights after pressing on your closed eyelids, and are the result of retinal excitation. Entoptic 'seeing' is the result of neuronal firing deeper within the visual system of the brain.[4]

Researcher Paul Devereux relates entoptic vision to the shaman in his book *Shamanism and the Mystery Lines: Ley Lines, Spirit Paths, Shape-Shifting* & *Out-of-body Travel*. He states that many past studies of the visionary deal with hallucinations that arose from drug intoxication and psychiatric conditions. Beginning in the nineteenth century, a group called the Club des Haschichins repeatedly reported images of whirlpools, spirals and rainbows from their investigation into stages of cannabis trances. In 1888, P. Max Simon studied schizophrenic hallucinations and discovered that patients' visions emphasized spider webs, ropes and meshes. Another researcher working in 1924 with cannabis noted patterns and cited crystals, stars and filigree lacework.

These patterns were finally classified in the work of Heinrich Klüver as 'form constants.' From 1926 to 1966, while working with mescaline imagery, Klüver contrived four categories of form constants: the lattice, the web, the tunnel or funnel and the spiral. Ronald K. Siegel and Murray E. Jarvik went on to recognize that form constants were part of a two-part process of hallucination, and they further expanded the categories of form constants in 1975. The first stage involved eight categories of form constants: lattices, webs, tunnels or funnels, spirals, lines, curves (and nesting curves), kaleidoscopes and random patterns. The second stage, which relates directly to the shamanic journey, occurred when these patterns merged with memories and from these, landscapes, people and buildings emerged out of the forms. J.D. Lewis-Williams and T.A. Dowson delineated a third stage of this hallucinatory process in 1988 when they included bodily sensation after the visual effects stage. It is interesting to note that researchers subsequent to Klüver found that form constants can also be induced through sensory deprivation, electronic brain stimulation, crystal gazing, and flashing lights—all elements that are known to help the shaman shift from ordinary consciousness to the shamanic state of consciousness.[5]

When I stumbled upon this information, it explained a personal experience I had written about in June of 1996.

Each of the last three evenings when we worked, I experienced a strange phenomenon as I initially closed my eyes for meditation. I would see an energy grid on my internal screen. One night it was repeating frogs; another night it was leaves; another, an indeterminate pattern. All reminded me of the nesting patterns of Escher. It was only after reflection that I recalled some of the same type of internally generated light grid experiences after using a friend's Hemi-sync® technology.

—Personal journal, Crestone, CO, June 1996

I had been at a weeklong conference that involved using a meditative state to attempt telepathy. We stayed up late, ate at unusual times and experienced some schedule disruptions. At the time I wondered about the origin of the visions. After reading Devereux I determined that my images were a kind of shamanic awakening to another way of perceiving. My note to myself next to the above journal entry was "these 'lights in my eyes'—phosphenes". As I review the experience now, I understand that it was entoptic vision giving way to form constants.

Continuing to track Devereux's historical quest, I read about the work of Celia Green. In 1968 she was conducting work on ecsomatic experience—that is, out-of-body experience. Out-of-body experiences, for the purpose of her research, were those experiences that come with sleep and dreaming. This relates to the shaman's ecstasy in which the shaman takes flight and travels during his explorations of the spirit worlds. The shaman is said to leave his body to journey. In working with out-of-body experience, Green coined the term 'metachoric' to describe the nature of the related hallucination: one that turns the entire ordinary waking conscious field of vision into a hallucination.[6] As a reminder, hallucination implies a visionary experience that doesn't originate outside or in front of the eyes. When this notion of an entire field of vision becoming a hallucination was applied to lucid dreaming, researcher Stephen LaBerge was able to talk about rolling out of his body and moving about his bedroom—during a lucid dream—as moving within the metachoric equivalent of his bedroom.[7] His body was at rest, but his awareness was active and moving through a landscape that was being perceived without the benefit of external stimuli—a metachoric landscape. A metachoric landscape is as real as any other; it occurs in non-ordinary reality and can impact the experiencer just as significantly as can an ordinary reality landscape.[8]

Tying these studies to the shaman we can understand that there is richness and even a scientific understanding for the shaman's visions. A word of caution, however. It is important to underscore a distinction made by Mircea Eliade: since hallucination can be applied to one who is psychotic, Eliade remarks that the shaman controls and makes use of the visions, while the psychotic cannot. The shaman moves into his ecstasy or altered state of consciousness via extreme pain, fear, fatigue, fasting, near-death, shock, hypoxia, sensory deprivation, meditation, or monotony. Some of the old time shamans really suffered for their experiences. Fortunately for us, the sonic driving of a drum can trigger the altered state and we can avoid such unattractive methods.

The shaman's perceptions of landscape often occur where there can be no external stimuli, such as in darkness or behind a veil. This is similar to my Crestone meditation experience that occurred in the dark and is similar to the Hemi-sync® format I used in which a mask shields the eyes and lights are flashed onto the closed eyelids. Both the darkness and the flashing lights produced lattice type grids—one of the form constants. It is interesting to note that the technique used to travel to the lower world is to follow a tunnel, another of the form constants.

During the shaman's journey, landscapes open to the shaman and become the stage upon which activity takes place according to what one knows of the world. If we borrow from Green, this landscape might be called a metachoric landscape. Castañeda calls it a "separate reality." A field of vision opens to the shaman that is not related to what is going on outside of or in front of the eyes. This landscape is every bit as real as the landscape external to the eye and often gives rise to very intense sensations and emotions. But is the journey of the shaman strictly an inward one, as all of this suggests?

Shamans from Siberia as well as other places describe their journeys as "flying off" into other worlds. Perhaps it is enough to know that a shift of attention is made from ordinary waking consciousness into the shamanic state of consciousness, during which objects such as landscapes, people and buildings can be perceived according to the vocabulary of one's personal experiences. Yet, this would not account for the access the shaman has to information unknown to him in ordinary reality while in the ecstatic state, particularly his ability to divine. Perhaps the final link is provided by recent science regarding the 'non-local mind.'

Research in quantum physics has demonstrated that awareness isn't limited by our physicality but rather can expand limitlessly beyond the braincase. In fact, physicist David Bohm has said that everything in the universe is part of a continuum; everything is in some way alive, imbued with intelligence and energy; and every portion of the universe enfolds the whole.[9] These ideas are the foundation of Michael Talbot's *The Holographic Universe*, a book that explains the mechanisms of divination from a scientific perspective. The universe can speak to the shaman through all things, since each component of the universe enfolds the whole and has intelligence. And perhaps it is through the apparent internal experience of the shaman that the shaman's awareness opens and expands to access outward realms where information can be received, processed and comprehended through the shaman's metaphoric interpretation of the metachoric. Perhaps this is how the shaman 'flies.'

Many of today's shamanic travelers use the drum as a tool to enter this expansive shamanic state of consciousness. Other sonic drivers are known in the shamanic world—for example, rattles, waterfalls and winnowing fans. Beyond sound, there is monotonous movement: stones to grind if you are an Eskimo and rice to pound if you are Japanese. These activities shift the state of consciousness out of the ordinary and allow for a different way of perceiving.

Dance is also a common consciousness-changing tool. From the !Kung in Africa we know of *num,* the healing energy raised to *kia* through dance.[10] These San people hold healing dances where the women sing and dance to stimulate the *num*. When this 'boiling energy' reaches a threshold, the dancer shifts into *kia*.[11] While in this non-ordinary state, healing is shared with the community through sweat rubbed from the dancer to others; dancers talk to the spirits, arguing for the well-being of the community; souls of the sick are pursued and retrieved.[12]

Voodoo also uses dance. Congo Square in New Orleans was well known through the 1800s for Sunday meetings of the Creoles—free born and slave, black and white—who would meet to dance and lose themselves in trance. One particular dance—the Conjure Dance—is still practiced today for compassionate and healing purposes in the context of community.[13]

Native Americans also have a long history of dance as a means to induce visionary states. Much of this can be traced through the prophets who were seeking peace after the white incursion. Probably the best known of these prophets was Wovoka, who initiated the Ghost Dance. This dance was inspired by a dream and was used as a ritual to enter ecstasy or trance. While in trance, participants were said to enter landscapes of plenty where they saw deceased friends and relatives.[14]

Even recently, body movement has been used to elicit changes in one's psycho-emotional state. Anthony Robbins, the popular motivational guru, challenges his students to change their states through awareness and changes in posture.[15] Through exercises in which pupils are asked to observe and move their bodies, posture and movement are presented as devices useful in creating particular emotional states. Another example is the intense body movement developed by famous Indian guru Osho as a way for Westerners—who tend to have a difficult time relaxing—to enter meditation. And, Felicitas Goodman has introduced the use of postures to initiate spirit journeys. Her work uses numerous body postures from non-Western art—such as figurines and rock paintings—to stimulate shifts in consciousness to the ecstatic trance and its visionary experience.[16]

Still other methods are used to enter altered states of consciousness. The Hindus and Buddhists use diagrams called mandalas. These intriguing and intricate forms are based on the metaphor of the circle and the center, inviting the observer to enter with the intention of going deeper or expanding outward to find wholeness.[17] Throughout the ages and cross-culturally, mandalas have been used for shifting into different levels of awareness. Many of them are reminiscent of kaleidoscopes, one of the form constants highlighted by Siegel and Jarvik.

Breath is also used to shift consciousness. Stanislov Grof began by studying LSD in the late 1960s and outlined similar stages of hallucination cited by Siegel and Jarvik as well as Lewis-Williams and Dowson. When the use of LSD for therapy became politically untenable in the 70s, Grof switched to Holotropic® Breathing as a means to initiate an altered state of consciousness. This use of the breath as a tool is rooted in the Indian Yogic tradition of *pranayama*.[18] Grof has used this breath-induced altered state of consciousness to help people access the non-local mind that connects all of existence in order to help people resolve personal challenges; in other words, to heal. According to Grof, access to the information within non-local mind through the breath provides information that can be physically and emotionally spectacular and profound.[19]

The shaman *sees* things on his or her flight that can be used to gain information that may or may not be in the normal, ordinary reality purview of the shaman. These things a shaman sees play out on a field of perception and pass through the shaman's own metaphoric system. What we know is that there are many ways to stimulate the shamanic state of consciousness and thereby induce visions. The threads of entoptic vision, form constants, metachoric landscapes and non-local mind weave together to create a tapestry that informs through metaphor. For the shaman, all that matters is that he or she is on a spirit journey and *knows*.

It is useful to step into an awareness of our individual states of consciousness and methods for achieving them. In the following Orient & Navigate you have the opportunity t o examine your triggers for various states and perhaps begin to understand more deeply how to apply this knowledge in various situations.

Orient & Navigate: The Metaphoric & Metachoric

Exercise #1: Personal Variations in Consciousness

As we go through our day we experience many states of consciousness. We begin our day rising from sleep, in which we may have been dreaming. We stumble through our morning routine, half asleep, relying on habit to shower, apply make-up and grab a bite to eat. We hit the gym and pump our bodies full of oxygen and are in a state of excitation. We drive to the office and wonder how we got there—must be autopilot. Each of these situations represents a subtle variation in consciousness.

Make a list of situations in which you are aware of a distinct tone of consciousness. Describe how your body feels in each of the situations. Which one is most relaxing? In which one are you most alert?

When you want to change your mental state, what, if anything, do you do with your body?

Orient & Navigate: The Metaphoric & Metachoric

Exercise #2: Sonic Drivers

Consider sound and how it can drive your mood.

When I think of sound as a sonic driver, I am immediately taken back to my childhood and the backseat of our Chevy Impala. As my dad would steer it along the New York State Thruway, I would be lulled into an altered state by the repetitive *ker-thump, ker-thump, ker-thump* of the tires passing over the seams of the concrete sections of the road. As a kid, I loved the floaty sensation that the steady thumping would produce.

What memories do you have of a sound connected to a state? It doesn't have to be 'floaty' or pleasant. For example, it could be a state of alert wariness induced by the discordant sound of a dental drill!

Exercise #3: Mood Music

We often use music to change our mood. Some music soothes and other music brings about a foul temper. Make a list of your favorite music (and not so favorite!) and associate it with a state or mood.

5 What is a Landscape?

Mystical practices and folk magic, in their earliest forms, grew out of the generations of human life in a specific geographic area and the relationship that evolved between humanity and the land, waterways and sky.
—Orion Foxwood, *The Faery Teachings*[1]

As shamanic explorers we look outside of our typical waking reality to find information beyond human ken. To get this knowledge we must go deeper, beyond our ordinary vision and attention. We go to the bare bones—the land. This is the land of the countryside, not the country. A country is crafted by humans and is the purview of politicians. Landscape is the land—its discernable features, its associated flora and fauna, and the mechanisms that created its features. We notice the curves, the folds, the lines, and the forms when we look at the physical world or the worlds we encounter during our shamanic journeys.

Landscape is the underlying stage on which our vision plays out. In the worlds of ordinary reality and non-ordinary reality, action takes place in a context that includes a landscape. Lines and curves resolve and we identify a landscape in which our presence makes us a participant in its energy and intelligence. Knowing this enables us to detect and interpret its influence upon us and act in accord with its messages.[2] Disciplines that contribute to our understanding of landscape include geology, physical geography, and ecology. The landscapes discussed in this book are not strictly defined geological formations but also include biomes—communities of plants and animals whose lives center on a dominant physical feature. For the shaman, all these things and their inter-relatedness are informative.

Landscapes can shake us up by warping our dimensional perception and making us think. I remember the story of a woman who couldn't wait to move back to the city from her house in the woods; she didn't like squirrels looking in the window at her. There are stories of pioneering women who went mad in the prairies because the vastness was impossible to mentally accommodate. Landscapes and the creatures associated with them cause us distress when they challenge our anthropocentric views. Redwood trees dwarf us. Against the rocky clitter (clitter is the stone that breaks off tors and litters moorland) of a moor, the lichen mocks us as mere babes. It is difficult to understand the truths held in landscapes—we are accustomed to thinking of ourselves as omnipotent. We race to retreat into our contrived spaces that isolate and protect us from the natural world.

There are those who are naturally attracted to the landscape. For them, communion with a rocky ridge is much easier than discourse with other humans. The sound of water lapping upon the shore of a lake is music and the vision of a desert at sunset, numinous. There are even others who will risk all and, in humility, enter dangerous landscapes—some to scale soaring mountains, some to dive deep into the abyss. These individuals are the Earth's great mediums, opening up to the enchantment of landscape and channeling tales to entice and enthrall us. Through them we develop the courage to step out from behind our protective shield of familiar space to explore the less traveled niches of our Great Spaceship Earth.

The physical sciences that have contributed to our ability to distinguish landscapes include geology, which deals with the structure of the earth's crust, and physical geography, which deals with the earth's natural features. These disciplines help us to understand the forces behind the scenes that create mountains, caverns and glaciers. The mystical language of these disciplines refers to erosion, subduction, water cycles and volcanism. Translated into the elementary language of the shaman, there are Air, Earth, Water and Fire.

Of Ratios and Spirals

The language of mathematics also contributes to our understanding, especially when considering what is meant by 'intelligence.' I have expressed throughout this book that there is intelligence in landscapes. The kind of intelligence I suggest and have appreciated in landscape has to do with a pervasive encoding that reflects order and awareness—two components I find essential to intelligence.

One demonstration of the deep encoding throughout the universe involves an examination of form. The ancients engaged in the study and use of sacred form for many thousands of years. When we talk of sacred form we are talking about structures and patterns that capture the relationship of one thing to another; for example, the symbolic language of mathematics. It has been widely recognized that there are consistent geometric patterns found in nature that are the building blocks of matter in our world, our universe. The 3-D patterns Western Culture is probably most familiar with are the five Platonic solids plus the sphere. These solids are: the cube, the tetrahedron, the octahedron, the icosahedron and the pentagonal dodecahedron. All of these solids can nest inside a sphere with their edges' points intersecting the surface of the sphere.[3] These shapes are the basis of structure and are seen most clearly in crystal and metal structures.

As we look at structure, these geometries and the algebraic expression of the structural relationships are represented by a constant called *phi* (pronounced 'fee'). *Phi* is the underlying constant that defines the Golden Rectangle that was the basis for the pleasing proportionality of Greek architecture.[4] The *Phi* Ratio is known in all organic structures.

Our bodies are encoded with the *Phi* Ratio. DaVinci's Canon, more correctly called *Vitruvian Man* or *Proportions of Man*, is DaVinci's drawing of a human inside a circle and a square. The *Phi* Ratio can be seen in the proportions such as the distance of the navel between the top of the head and bottom of the feet; the length of the hand and the bone of the forearm; the length of the foot and the tibia, to name a few.[5] Animals also are 'built' according to the *Phi* Ratio.

Phi is a ratio that defines the Golden Mean rectangle, which in turn defines the Golden Mean spiral. This form was seen by the Greeks as the ideal and thus is connected to or actually as 'God.' As a spiral, the form has no beginning and no end—extends infinitely inward and infinitely outward—and is thus an ideal representation in this sense. As we begin to include 'God' in the equation, we begin to grasp 'presence' or 'awareness'; something had to establish this order, this perfection.

There is another sequence or mathematical relationship that expresses a spiral nature. It is the Fibonacci sequence: 1, 1, 2, 3, 5, 8, 13, 21, 34, 55, 89. . . This sequence expresses a spiral, with a fixed beginning. It is a very close approximation of *phi* as the spiral moves outward. Some examples of the Fibonacci spirals in nature are pine cone seeds and the fruitlets of a pineapple.[6]

As we continue to look at spirals in our universe, they can be mathematically languaged and that language can be expanded to encompass the encoding of light, sound, musical harmonies, and life—its form and structure—especially when coupled with an understanding of the Platonic solids. We see spirals in galaxies and the electromagnetic field of the human heart. Because these geometries are so powerful and fundamental to our understanding of life and our evolution, we call them sacred. In this context, sacred connotes a connection to creation and the Divine. This is what is meant by intelligence—order and awareness.

Thus, behind the workings of Air, Earth, Water and Fire, there is order and awareness. Air carries sound in waves and spirals; Earth grows crystals in Platonic solids; Water flows in waves and currents; Fire—in the form of electromagnetism—moves in waves and spirals. Waves, light and motion can all be mathematically represented. Working in a shamanic way we attempt to establish a relationship with the intelligence of each in order to work with it, to enlist its support. To do so, we must first acknowledge the existence of each—Air, Earth, Water and Fire—and show respect. We are beginners.

The Makers

The Makers—Air, Earth, Fire and Water—are more than mere mechanisms of erosion and deposition. They are powerful forces of intelligence that work independently and in concert with one another to shape the ground of our support—a thin crust of a earth and water that covers the globe like a film of shrink wrap around a beach ball mostly filled with molten rock. Air surrounds us and is the breath of life and inspiration. As a Maker, Air is the wind that carves windows into rocks and cliffs into hoodoos. It is Air that carries the clouds that race across the sky. Air is sound, vibrations and silence, and we can learn much from the dust devil Air whips up from the desert or the gentle tug upon our hair at the beach.

Water makes up most of our bodies. It is the pelting force of rain, the flowing power of the river and the grinding force of a glacier. Still water, flowing water, tides, currents, waves. Water dissolves rock. All this water-motion works upon the surface of the land, sculpting it, shaping it and transforming it—moment to moment. Water can move quickly, as in a tidal surge, or move patiently, as in the slow drip-drip that over hundreds of years makes a stalagmite.

Fire bums in us. The Vedic scholars call it *agni*. We digest and fire consumes. Electric nerve impulses are fire racing through our bodies conveying signals along axons. Lightning strikes a prairie, driving life underground as the first step in renewal. Rock at the core of the earth is fiery and explodes through volcanoes and oozes from deep-sea trenches, making changes in an instant, or pushing continental shelves at a snail's pace. Sunlight is the greatest fire, for without it, there would be no life.

Earth is the rock, the foundation, the solidity upon which we tread. It folds, shakes, bumps and scours. Drops, rises, thrusts and sinks. At the level of ingredients, Earth is minerals, soil, and vegetal matter. Earth is the sphere whirling through space and the grains of sand carried on the wind, carving exposed stones into ghostly figures. Earth is pressure that moves continents and sedimentation that builds up deltas. These forces of intelligence are all active to varying degrees in each landscape, and the shaman has much to learn from them. The Makers aren't nouns, but verbs, full of action.

There is much interplay, too, in the betwixt and between places of landscape. The liminal comes into play as we find ourselves at doorways leading from one world to another, oftentimes being in neither or in both. Standing on the shore one can be in the ocean and/or on the beach. On a slope, one can be in the valley and/or on a mountain. The magic comes in the interface and the sudden shifts of perspective, when attention is moving from one form to another. This can be likened to the gap that one seeks in meditation: the place where infinite possibilities reside. Don Juan was speaking of the power of the betwixt and between when he told Carlos Castañeda that "twilight is the crack between the worlds."[7] The world has a special potency during liminal times, twilight and pre-dawn, when it is neither night nor day. We can experience a similar potency when we explore the threshold places between landscapes and between the worlds of ordinary and non-ordinary reality.

All of this may seem prosaic until we consider that these same concepts apply to the Lower, Middle and Upper Worlds of the shaman. The landscapes of these worlds also have Makers, whose visage and participation may vary from landscape to landscape but who are nevertheless always in attendance. As we work with each landscape, we will encounter the Makers and discover their roles in creation and the ways they inform us.

Guardians and Keepers

There are other organizing forces at work within landscapes that we call Guardians and Keepers. For our purposes a Guardian is the archetype or template of a given form of landscape, while a Keeper is the local expression of the form. For example, there is the Mountain Guardian that underlies or oversees all mountains. There is a specific Keeper of Mt. Washington. In approaching landscapes for information, there is an opportunity to contact both a Guardian and a Keeper. As you work with each landscape in ordinary and non-ordinary reality, you will make your own discoveries and build your own relationships with the Guardians and Keepers. The point in landscape work, both in ordinary and non-ordinary reality, is to pay attention to the land. Its forms and its inhabitants are a part of our grand adventure of life on Earth and have messages and meaning for us if we but take the time to connect and listen—not for what we expect to hear, but rather for what they have to say to us. When we quiet ourselves and open to the communication from the land's Guardians and Keepers—when we feel the tug of the wind, hear the words spoken by water, respond to the push or pull of heat and settle into the surety of the ground—we may be changed, touched or moved. This is the moment when we have crossed the threshold into the sacred.

As a reminder, simply because a place is important to a group or person doesn't mean that it is held as sacred. For the Penan, places that 'store' genealogies have nothing to do with the Divine or numinous, but are nevertheless significant. The fact that something of historical interest has happened at a particular location doesn't make that place sacred either. As Mark N. Trahant has commented, "[there's a] difference between a sacred place and a historical marker."[8] A place is sacred when it becomes entwined not only with our personal story, but also with our understanding of and proper relationship to all of creation and the Divine.

Beyond Makers, Guardians and Keepers

Marko Pogačnik is a devoted worker with land and the intelligence embodied within it. In this sense, Pogačnik not only recognizes an overarching order and awareness, but also individual, localized expressions of intelligence. Through his extraordinary vision, and the help of his talented children, he has outlined a 'sacred geography' that challenges us to engage with landscape in a significant way. In his book *Sacred Geography,* he takes us ever more deeply into the vital energetic systems of our Earth, highlighting Earth's breathing systems, centers of grounding, Yin-Yang systems, vital energy systems, heart centers and more. His sight illuminates for us these component systems of the *holon,* a unit within a given landscape that contains "vital-energy streams, consciousness networks, and a multitude of pieces of solid matter…permeable, multilayer[ed]."[9] Through his work, contact with the intelligence beyond the bodily structures of space and time is accomplished via the recognition of three other dimensions of reality: the soul dimension, the dimension of consciousness and the etheric dimension. Each of these dimensions manifests in patterns and systems upon our Earth. Each is affected by human action. Each requires attention, and oftentimes help, to function properly. In cases where he has found distress within a given *holon,* Pogačnik makes corrections using stones with designs carved upon them (called cosmograms) in an Earth-acupuncture practice he calls lithopuncture.[10]

This chapter began with a discussion of 'landscape.' When we examine the 'bare bones,' we find that there is more than meets our casual eye. In the following Orient & Navigate you will meet a challenge; how well do you know the landscape you inhabit?

Orient & Navigate: What is a Landscape?

Exercise #1: Describing

Think about the place where you live. How would you describe the land underfoot?

List as many descriptors as you can without actually using a landscape signifier. For example, if you live on a river bank you might say: sloping, damp, narrow, long, hard. Avoid saying 'river bank.' To accurately do this, you might have to physically be on the land. When you walk or bicycle, you have a greater appreciation for changes in elevation; a flat place in a car can be very hilly when you're pedaling.

Some useful descriptors: hard, soft, airy, slippery, smooth, rough, sandy, powdery, spongy, lumpy, earthy, moldy, salty, humid, hot, cold, quiet, dripping, cracking, open, vast, broad, enclosed, undulating, high, low, tall, short, curved, hilly, flat. Feel free to add your own.

Orient & Navigate: What is a Landscape?

 Exercise # 2: Mapping

Without consulting a topographical map, draw a map of where you live. Start small and map what would be a square mile with your house as the center. Eliminate streets and include only landscape features like rivers, streams, hills, mountains. Begin by making an 'X' for where you live and work from there.

Now consult a map and see how closely your map resembles the actual location of features upon the land.

What was easy to plot on your map?

What did you struggle to place on your map?

What thoughts crossed your mind as you worked on your map?

What did you have to use to orient yourself to the space and place; what were your reference points?

What did you learn about orienting yourself upon the land?

Orient & Navigate: What is a Landscape?

Exercise #3: The Language of Sensing

Pick a feature in the area near your home that you identified for Exercise #2: Mapping. Visit the spot either physically or in your mind using your memory and imagination. Notice what is on, near, in or adjacent to the feature. Begin to sense if there is interaction between the feature and the other objects, be they another feature or something manmade. Write your impressions of this interaction using only words that express an emotion or emotional quality.

Some useful descriptors: happy, sad, frightened, honored, overwhelmed, apprehensive, familiar, lonely, cheerful, anxious, intimidated, amazed, awed, depressed, alert, bored, interested, angry, nervous, surprised, pleased, dizzy, tense, reverent, anticipatory. Feel free to add your own.

Date:

Feature:

Emotional Impressions:

Orient & Navigate: What is a Landscape?

Exercise #4: Heart Sensing

Close your eyes and scan your body. See if you can locate the center of your awareness. For many people, it sits in the head or behind the eyes. Wherever you find this seat of your awareness, gently begin to move it to your heart center. It can rise on a balloon or it can descend in an elevator. When you feel that your awareness has settled in the area of your heart, repeat the previous exercise. You may use the same feature or you may pick another one.

Date:

Feature:

Emotional/Heart-Centered Impressions:

Was this exercise different from the previous one? How?

Try using other parts of your body to sense features and relationships between them and other objects/features. Record your impressions.

6 The Work of the Shaman: Journeying & Divination

The three cosmic levels - earth, heaven, underworld - have been put in communication . . . this communication is sometimes expressed through the image of a universal pillar, axis mundi, which at once connects and supports heaven and earth and whose base is fixed in the world below . . .
—Mircea Eliade, *The Sacred and the Profane*[1]

The Journey

One of the ways a person can discover information not readily in her conscious awareness is through the shamanic journey—a specialized form of divination. Since the publication of *The Way of the Shaman* by Michael Harner, many people who are keen to discover hidden knowledge have learned to journey in order to connect with helping spirits and acquire information.

The journey has been called the defining act of a shaman. The scholar on the leading edge of this view was Mircea Eliade, who referred to the intentional change in consciousness—that is, the journey—as *ecstasy*. Harner agreed with Eliade's emphasis on the importance of journeying until recently when, in *Cave and Cosmos*, he recognized that in "some indigenous societies, there are shamans who do not journey at all, and others who journey only in the Middle World or, if they journey beyond the Middle World, may not go to both the Upper and Lower Worlds."[2] He emphasized that for all shamans there is a "disciplined interaction with spirits in nonordinary reality to help and heal others."[3] Thus, the Mongolian shaman I mention in Chapter 2, who calls the spirits to her and is not journeying to them, would be considered a shaman by this expanded view. Regardless of labels, we as humans have the ability to journey to separate realities and interact directly with spirits.

So, what are these other worlds to which a shaman travels? Many shamanic cultures speak of a World Tree that connects the three worlds that make up the Universe: the Lower, Middle and Upper Worlds. This tree is often represented as a pole or post that rises up from a yurt in Siberia, or a *rewe*—a kind of ladder outside a shaman's home in Chile, for example. These are tangible representations of the indigenous shaman's ability to move between the worlds.

Each of these worlds has a mode of access and is a space and place in which the spirits interact with the shaman or journeyer.

The Lower World

To access the Lower World, one has to descend. This raises some eyebrows, especially for those of us brought up in traditions that connect 'down' to hell-fire and damnation. Pushing against this prejudice, we can open space around this constrictive viewpoint when we step away from our religious training for a different perspective.

One such perspective comes to us from the literature of our Western World: *Alice in Wonderland*. Alice tumbles into a rabbit hole and descends into a world of wonder she finds populated with fascinating creatures—both animal and human.

The Brothers Grimm collected the folk tale of Mother Holle who, likewise, lived in the land below. In this tale, two sisters experienced adventures after falling into a well and landing in the world below. The good sister did good deeds for those she met and was rewarded for her kindness by Mother Holle for whom she swept and cleaned. Upon her return to the ordinary world, Mother Holle showered the girl with gold pieces. Her lazy sister, feigning goodness, entered the well in order to reap the same golden gain. Her pretense of goodness soon faded. When her lazy ways resumed, Mother Holle sent her home. Rather than a shower of gold, the lazy sister was showered with pitch—impossible to remove.[4]

The idea of 'pitch' suggests to us some of the punitive aspects we associate with the Lower World. The tale makes it clear, however, that the punishment isn't doled out irrespective of one's nature; it is one's nature and how one lives it that initiates the consequences. Better life choices equal better results.

This applies directly to Lower World stories as the place of the afterlife. The Underworld or the Netherworld, as it is also called, was made up of several realms for the Greeks: Tartarus, home of damned souls; Asphodel Meadows, ruled by Hades and home to neutral souls; Isles of the Blessed (also Elysian Fields), ruled by Cronus and home to heroes; and, another aspect of the Elysian Fields, ruled by Rhadamanthys, home to the virtuous and initiates in the mysteries.

For the Welsh, *Annwn* is the Underworld. It is the place of the ancestors.[5] Prior to Christianity, it was a world of delights. Afterward, it was simply a place for the dead. For the Saorans, a hill tribe of India, the Under World was the destination of deceased souls. It was the dwelling place of the tutelary spirits and ancestors, governed by the tutelaries who also maintain important relations with the living.[6]

When accessing the Lower World, the modern journeyer often changes consciousness using a drumbeat or some other monotonous percussion. As discussed in Chapter 4, there are other methods for achieving a shift in consciousness, but the drumbeat combines simplicity, safety and effectiveness. One typically assumes a physical position conducive to journeying such as lying down on one's back with the eyes covered. A familiar ordinary reality opening into the earth is called to mind: a small or large rodent hole, a cave entrance, a subway entrance, a storm sewer opening or manhole cover, a hole in a tree, a hollowed out tree stump, or a place where water comes up out of the ground. To the beat of the drum, one enters the visualized starting point with as much awareness as possible. As *Star Trek's* Jean-Luc Picard might say, "make it so," using memory and imagination. This is an act of will. Once situated inside the opening, one moves downward through a tunnel, the tunnel to the Lower World. This tunnel may be composed of any of a number of materials. While it is an important zone of transition, the objective is not to remain in the tunnel, but rather to use it as a conduit to reach the world that waits below. Often, there is a light at the end of the tunnel. Sometimes, the descent is challenging, and one must use one's ingenuity or even ask for help in getting to the exit.[7]

Once in the Lower World, one may encounter a wide variety of experiences and landscapes. The Lower World may be visited by the shaman as he attempts to recover a patient's lost soul or lost power, or meets with her animal spirit helper, or helps the spirit of a deceased person find a suitable resting place. A place of wonder, incredible beauty, and unequivocal support, the Lower World rests patiently and eternally, awaiting our forays, ever ready to enlighten us and bestow its loving embrace upon us.

The Middle World

The Middle World can be described as the spiritual aspect of the world in which we live. It exists in parallel to our own—accessible with but a shift in our attention. A spirit has been defined as anything we 'see' with our eyes closed. To view the Middle World, close your eyes and look. On a journey into the Middle World, one's starting point is the body. Assume a journeying position and cover the eyes. To the beat of the drum, one moves out from the physical body in memory and imagination into the world in which we live via the back of a favorite spirit animal or by means of walking, running or flying.[8]

The shaman makes use of Middle World visions in removing harmful spirit intrusions from a patient's body, in finding lost objects or locating a wandering herd of game, in psychopomp work (helping the spirit of a deceased person to move on), or seeking help from the spirits of the natural world. Some have said that if danger exists in the spirit world, it is in the Middle World. On the other hand, the shaman is the one who goes where ordinary people refuse to go. The Middle World is the palette upon which the shaman paints his adventures and expresses her overflowing heart through which the great Red River of life flows.

The Upper World

The Upper World is Heaven, Asgard, Oz, Olympus, the Happy Hunting Ground. Multi-tiered, as is the Lower World, it is home to great and powerful spirits that some call gods and goddesses, others call saints or teachers. Our familiarity with stories of the Upper World calls to mind incredible lands, talking animals, beanstalks and giants, amazing monumental architecture, challenge, support and certainly fear, and a Supreme Being First Cause. Do we come from the Upper World, and do we ultimately return to it? Some have said that journeying to this realm and meeting a tutelary spirit there changes one's life forever.

There are many ways to access the Upper World. We have tales in our own culture that give us clues: Dorothy reached Oz by way of a tornado; Jack climbed a beanstalk; Jacob used a ladder. Outside our Western framework, Polynesian shamans use rainbows. Some Chinese and Korean shamans climb ladders made of swords. The Mapuche shamans of Chile mount the *rewe*, a notched pole. Popular culture also has made suggestions: Led Zeppelin sings of the stairway to heaven; Steppenwolf has a magic carpet ride. Other methods include rising on smoke exiting a fireplace or campfire; ascending on a geyser; jumping off a tree, building, or mountain and flying upward; rocketing up on the space shuttle or hopping aboard an elevator and pressing the appropriate button: Upper World 1.

Once again, one lies supine and rides the drumbeat—upward this time—using the chosen approach. Rising up, one will encounter a membrane. This membrane is not there to prevent entrance, but rather to delineate the threshold to the Upper World. This membrane may be as wispy as a cloud or as substantial as glass. One is a magician on the journey using whatever means is necessary to pass through the membrane. One can ask for an animal spirit helper to break through or materialize a tool to cut, saw or dig for access. In Siberia, the shaman's drum and drumstick were the personal tools of the shaman and could easily transform to become anything the shaman might need in the course of his journey. Once the membrane is open, one passes through it and begins the exploration of the Upper World.[9]

We can meet ancestors in the Upper World; we can seek healing for others or ourselves from the great helpers who reside there; we can interact with any who have come before us. We can come face to face there with our Oversoul, our own personal spiritual headquarters. The possibilities are limitless.

In journeying, the discipline is to always return to the starting point. It is essential that one completely returns. The shaman tells us that we have eternity to spend in the spirit world, but only a short time to spend in the physical world. It is in the physical world that we can effect changes and make miracles. The spirits of the Lower, Middle and Upper Worlds offer their great and loving help; all we need to do is accept it.

Some Guidelines for Your Journeys

In any journey you take, you will be using a sonic driver. In the aforementioned instructions, a drum is used. It is preferable that you have your full attention on the journey. This will require a drumming CD, download, or an actual drummer. In any case, the drumming will be steady for an allotted period, usually 10-30 minutes, and include a signal termed a callback to let you know your time in non-ordinary reality is ending. The callback is a change in rhythm and lets you know that it is time to retrace your tracks back through your entry and home to your starting point and physical body.

Initial journeys are often filled with the static of doubt. People wonder how much is imagination and how much is real. The word imagination isn't one that runs afoul to the journey. In fact, it is a primer that can initiate the movement of one's awareness or spirit body into the other realms. Best practice at the onset is to imagine a bucket at your side before you begin a journey. Take five deep balancing breaths, and as you do so, deposit all your doubts and worries of the day into the bucket, promising yourself that you can retrieve them upon your return. Then use your will and intention to initiate movement. Just as you can lift your arm by needing to scratch your head, so too can you move into the tunnel or fly up through the membrane. Once through the transition zones, your relaxed yet aware state prepares you to perceive the landforms and beings of the other realms.

I used to expect that once the drumming started, the movie of the week would appear. That was not the case. I had to use my own volition to enter the tunnel or to begin the ascent and continue moving. I learned to aid myself with questions, self-coaching. I'd enter the tunnel and ask myself, "What does this feel like?" An answer would come to me immediately and I'd use it to reinforce what I perceived. The answers to similar sensory questions helped focus my journeys and kept me alert as I moved through the Upper, Middle and Lower Worlds.

Repetition builds familiarity with the territories of the journey; the doubts drop away and the path becomes well-marked and clear. Eventually you, like the shaman, know the way. Remember, as a journeyer you must initiate movement. Once you begin to perceive the landscapes of the worlds, things will begin to happen that are beyond the limits of your mind.

Being well rested is important in journeywork. Fatigue combined with listening to a drumbeat and lying down in darkness can lead rapidly to a nap. If sleep continually overtakes you while you are trying to journey, there are a couple of remedies. The first is to change your journeying position. Lying down is not mandatory. Sit up or stand, if you prefer. It is even possible to journey while moving. There are many cross-cultural examples of shamans who move, dance and leap while 'shamanizing.' Sip a cup of green tea. Try different times of day. Although most shamans work at night, morning may be best for you. The most obvious though is to get more sleep.

Another frequent concern of journeyers is which world to visit for what purpose. Building relationships with helpful animal spirits can alleviate this concern; one learns to meet them in non-ordinary reality and trust their lead as they direct or accompany us on journeys. Certain cultures have specific purposes associated with each world. For the Khanty, a group in Western Siberia, the Lower World is where the healer goes to retrieve a lost soul; the Middle World is where the shaman acts to remove spiritual causes of pain and illness; the Upper World is where the shaman meets the gods and works toward resolution of communal afflictions.[10] In core shamanism, the non-culturally specific practice, these activities can take place in any of the worlds and each journeyer develops personal methodologies.

Divination

Divination, as we learned from Jaynes, doesn't always rely on the shamanic journey. In fact, the shamanic journey is but one type or form of divination. There are many examples of divinatory methods employed across the globe. The Saorans, a group from India, would wave a lamp over a patient. Where the flame of the lamp flared up over the body was an indication of trouble.[11] In Cameroon and Nigeria, a spider was left under a pot with some stones, sticks and a stack of cards. Left to its own devices for a time, the spider moved the material. When exposed, the placement of the stones, sticks and cards revealed a message.[12]

We can move beyond augury into a broader experience with more possibilities when we engage in spontaneous divination. Approaching the land with a question or concern, we are met with intelligence that we can absorb and decipher. This revelatory experience happens with resonance and compassion. In our authentic need, the spirits of place respond. The nature of our resonance determines the means of response. In other words, our question is put forth and the resonance of the question is matched by the spirits. They reveal themselves in a way that uses the vocabulary of our personal experience. This is the personal metaphor. Once received, we can then translate the metaphor into an understandable, useable answer.

Formulating Questions

At the root of all divination work, including the journey, is a question. We all seek insights and answers to our mysteries. Anthony Robbins has said, "If you want a good answer, you have to ask a better question."[13]

Grade school recollections will remind us of who, what, when, where, why and how. Let's examine and evaluate each as tools for good journey and divination questions.

Who?

Questions that begin with 'who' can be tricky. Most of us are not entirely ego-free and will oftentimes ask questions using 'who' for which we have some pretty strong notions. "Who will hire me?" "Who will give me a million dollars?" The 'who' in the answer to these types of questions may not even be known. We can struggle with our analytical mind to get an answer while fighting an expectation—it's got to be Joe because he's the only millionaire I know.

What?

'What' is an excellent beginning to a journey or divination question. "What do I need to know now?" "What can I do to best help Jane?" These are the kind of open-ended questions that can yield startling results.

When?

Of all the questions, 'when' is the least productive. Time in non-ordinary reality does not progress at the same rate or in the same manner as it does in ordinary reality. Non-ordinary reality is outside of space and time as we understand these dimensions. Asking for the date that your ship will come in or when you'll meet the love of your life will only lead to disappointment. It's not that the spirits are unable to communicate 'when'; it is simply that their 'when' and our 'when' don't necessarily track. If you need to ask a question that involves a notion of timing (e.g., "When will I meet the person who will teach me to quilt?"), better to ask it in another form such as, "What can I do to meet the person who can teach me to quilt?"

Where?

These questions can be very interesting. Sometimes, like a 'who' question, a 'where' can be clouded with too many expectations. However, it still is a valid form, unlike a 'when' question. "Where will I find my life partner?" "Where is my lost ring?" Details arising from journeying with these types of questions may very well lead the querent to fruitful ends.

Why?

When I consider 'why,' I am reminded of an adage from *est*, the training developed by Werner Erhard. In his not so delicate way he said, "Understanding in life is the booby prize." 'Why' is a question that may lead to understanding, but the energy stops there. Understanding why I always procrastinate or why my daughter is angry may not solve the problem. Better questions would be: "What can I do to stop procrastinating?" or "How can I help my daughter diffuse her anger?"

How?

This is the muscle question. 'How' seeks a prescription for action that can instigate a change or a new understanding." How can I get more energy?" "How can I start a new business?" "How do I communicate better with my father?"

Yes/No, Should, Either/Or

Two other question pitfalls are worth mentioning. The first is the 'Yes/No' question that simply yields "Yes" or "No" as an answer. As mentioned earlier in Chapter 2, sortilege is a kind of binary divination. One asks a question, flips a coin and gets an answer. The answer may be informative, but only in a limited way. The journey and other forms of divination can provide much more information. You may consider asking a broader question. For example, "Should I go to law school?" could be changed to "What are the advantages of going to law school?" or "What do I need to know about going to law school?" And, what about 'Should' questions? 'Should' implies compliance with the will of the spirits. In my view, we work best when we work together to co-create; we are better served—spirit allies and humans—by keeping the 'shoulding' to a minimum. A version of the 'Yes/No' is the 'Either/Or' choice. Chicago or Cleveland? Bob or Ted? Consider asking "Where is the best place to go to school?" or "What do I need to know when choosing the best person for my chess team?" Expand the possibilities in your question for richer answers.

Another bit of advice concerns the complexity of questions. When one settles in to take a journey or perform a divination, the temptation is to really get a bang for your buck. Resist that temptation and keep the questions simple. The spirits know you and all your considerations.

Just ask the question. One per journey or divination session usually works best. If you get an answer you don't understand, ask for clarification. If you get an answer that requires a second question, take another journey or set aside time for another divination session and ask the second question. Keep your question, your intention for the journey or divination, precise and clear. This will help you focus and remember the visions and information that arise.

Topics for Questions

What are some possibilities for questions? *Feng shui* is helpful in guiding us to consider all the possibilities. In this ancient system, a *bagua* is placed over a room as a map. This eight-sided figure delineates the areas of human life that are affected by the real world components of a room. It is a comprehensive model and useful for us as we think about what to ask in a divinatory exercise. While it is not the purpose of this book to delve into the many aspects of *feng shui*—that could take lifetimes to fully appreciate as a highly specialized method to read the energies of place and space—using the *bagua* to suggest topics for divinatory query is a way to honor this ancient practice and to illuminate human concerns worthy of exploration and spiritual help. What follows below are the *bagua* categories.

A thought as you develop your question: make it something that really matters to you. A concern that has 'juice,' emotionality and vibrancy sets up the resonance necessary for a clear, strong reply. And a moment for ethics: we only journey and divine for ourselves unless we have permission to do so on another's behalf. As journeyers and diviners we don't fix things or put in our 'two cents' unless we are specifically asked to do so.

Bagua Categories—Query Possibilities[14]

Career: This area concerns the ways in which you use your talents, the directions in which you apply your abilities. It concerns your occupation but also your interests and hobbies. It deals with all the avenues for your passion, paid or otherwise.

Knowledge: Knowledge includes formal education, licensure and certification. It also includes higher spiritual knowledge, the education of your children, and how you share knowledge.

Family: The issues in this category primarily center on the family of origin and the extended family. Secondarily included are broader group dynamics: clubs, work groups and teams, for example.

Wealth: This is money into your financial system and money out. Consider wages, lotteries, inheritance, stocks, gifts, expenses, charities, and retirement funds.

Fame & Reputation: Issues governed by this area concern your image, how people perceive you. This area addresses the ways you can become known for what you do (marketing), your self-expression and your relationship to the world.

Partnership: All sorts of partnerships are considered here: personal partners (spouse, friend), business partners, spiritual partners. Think, too, of how you partner with yourself to reach your highest potential.

Children & Creativity: One's own children are covered in this category, but also included are the fruits of creativity—projects like books, music or art. Remember the children in your neighborhood and don't forget your inner child

Helpful People: These are the relationships that stand outside the circle of partnership but are still critical for your support. They can be professionals who repair your home or ease your soul (roofer, minister). They are friends who carpool with you, clients who bring you business. They are benefactors and angels. They are your network and resources.

Health: This area concerns all areas of health: physical, mental, emotional and spiritual. It is about balance and well-being.

In the following Orient & Navigate exercises, divination activities are presented for your exploration. An example is provided to give you a feel for the discipline involved in divination—that is, the discipline necessary to arrive at a useful, understandable, relevant answer. Use the *bagua* categories above to form your own concise questions.

The following exercises and forms for recording your answers may be used repeatedly. As a reminder and hint: photocopy the worksheets and glue them into your journal. Glue sticks are great! This will give you a fresh page to record your work each time you practice. Date your work, too. If you choose to work on a particular issue over time, you may discover a shift in your awareness or attitude toward the issue that you can track via the date.

Orient & Navigate: The Work of the Shaman: Journeying & Divination

To begin to stretch our divining muscles, there are a series of exercises below. Each divination exercise will begin with a question. Using the bagua model, determine the question you will be taking out into the world. Take a journal and pen with you, as you may wish to record the answers and thoughts that come to you.

Divination performed in the following exercises is very subtle. A Native American teacher put it this way: "Don't be so busy looking for the whirlwind that you miss the breeze." This is an important lesson for all of us who live in the modern world of better, more, bigger, nicer. Divination is about slowing down and opening to the world. Allow plenty of time to practice each exercise.

Exercise #1: Clouds

Riding above the landscape on the Maker Air are wonderful sculptures built out of the Maker Water. Who cannot recall lazy childhood afternoons gazing up to find circus animals in the clouds? This exercise is a return to that time of innocence.

Formulate your question and go out to the sky. Watch the clouds and see if one or more of them resembles something, a bird for example. When you have discovered some form or other in the clouds, write it down in your journal and ask yourself: "What is it about this form that evokes an answer to my question?" Ask this question seven times and write the answers. These seven answers will provide insights you may not have considered.

Example: My question is: What can I do to enforce seat time for writing? After gazing at the sky I see a cloud that resembles a *zeuglodon*. I write down 'zeuglodon' in my journal. I then engage in stream of consciousness about zeuglodons, noting what stands out. Having become familiar with the zeuglodon as a sea wolf, wasgo or water dragon, I know that this prehistoric creature has a mouth full

Orient & Navigate: The Work of the Shaman: Journeying & Divination

of teeth and a snake-like neck and flippers. It lived in the water and some think the Loch Ness monster is its present-day kin. I let this knowledge sink in and then pull out seven of the most prominent characteristics or qualities that strike me from my musings: teeth, predatory, immersed in water, prehistoric, Sea Wolf, Nessie and swimming. Then I work the metaphor.

Note: Working with many people during a divinatory process, I have learned that it is best to take the question and make it a declarative sentence with appropriate blanks to get a good answer. For example, my question is made into such a sentence this way: Using the idea of (insert the characteristic/quality), I can enforce seat time for writing by _____. This helps you to stay on track. When you've worked the metaphor completely, the answer will sing. The point is that your answer and sentence have to make some kind of sense and address the question.

1. teeth

Using the idea of 'teeth,' I can enforce seat time for writing by sinking my teeth into what I am doing.

Notice that I answered the question in a full sentence using the model from above. The answer to how does a zeuglodon answer my question wasn't 'teeth.' It was a fully developed sentence that informs me that I must get really involved in my writing. Puns, sayings and adages can play a role in working the answers.

2. predatory (The zeuglodon's jaw filled with teeth makes me think of predators. Predators are often territorial.)

Using the idea of 'predatory,' I can enforce seat time for writing by setting aside a time and place to write and defend the time and place as a predator defends territory.

Orient & Navigate: The Work of the Shaman: Journeying & Divination

3. immersed in water

Using the idea of 'immersed in water,' I can enforce seat time for writing by immersing myself in a subject that sustains and excites me.

4. prehistoric (This word/idea deals with the past.)

Using the idea of 'prehistoric,' I can enforce seat time for writing by using a practice that has worked to enforce seat time in the past.

5. Sea Wolf (The sea wolf is another name for the zeuglodon and also the name of an AA hockey league. When I was following the Mississippi Sea Wolves, they won many a game with persistence.)

Using the idea of 'Sea Wolf,' I can enforce seat time for writing by being persistent and keeping the completed project or goal in mind.

6. Nessie (The zeuglodon has an appearance that has many thinking that the Loch Ness monster is a modern day specimen. The Loch Ness monster reminds me of the world beyond logic, a world of magic, mystery and spirits.)

Using the idea of Nessie, I can enforce seat time for writing by asking for the help of my helping spirits and the Creator for discipline and inspiration.

7. swimming (The zeuglodon I saw in the clouds appeared to be diving into the waves--swimming. Swimming is an exercise. Seat time is easier if I have exercised.)

Using the idea of swimming, I can enforce seat time for writing by exercising before sitting to write.

Orient & Navigate: The Work of the Shaman: Journeying & Divination

Now I have seven answers to my question—all are great answers and worthy of implementation. There is no conflict among the seven, although on occasion there may be. Consider conflicting answers an opportunity to think outside of the box.

Note: It's a good idea to date your readings so that you can trace the usefulness of your answers over time. Some teachers of divination who use the *I Ching* suggest waiting three months before asking the same question. This makes sense as it gives answers and adjustments time to ripen.

Orient & Navigate: The Work of the Shaman: Journeying & Divination

Exercise #1: Clouds

Date:

Your Question:

What you see in the clouds:

Stream of consciousness about image:

1:
Thoughts & Metaphoric Connections:

Using the idea of _____,

2:
Thoughts & Metaphoric Connections:

Using the idea of _____,

3:
Thoughts & Metaphoric Connections:

Using the idea of _____,

4:
Thoughts & Metaphoric Connections:

Orient & Navigate: The Work of the Shaman: Journeying & Divination

Using the idea of _____,

5:
Thoughts & Metaphoric Connections:

Using the idea of _____,

6:
Thoughts & Metaphoric Connections:

Using the idea of _____,

7:
Thoughts & Metaphoric Connections:

Using the idea of _____,

Orient & Navigate: The Work of the Shaman: Journeying & Divination

Exercise #2: Walking the Compass

Traditions world-wide have understood that each of the directions has an associated teaching, qualities and characteristics that resonate with a seeker. Not all traditions agree on the same teachings of East, South, West and North, but they do recognize the balance that comes from building on the knowledge and wisdom gleaned from them all.

Often people will speak of the Medicine Wheel as a tool to explore the various lessons of the directions. In one practice of the Medicine Wheel, thirty six stones are placed upon the ground to hold space for the points on the compass, the elements, four clans, the Sun, the Moon, the Earth and pathways to the cardinal points or directions.[15]

We will be working with the pathways to the cardinal directions.

The East is known as the place of illumination.[16] It is associated with mental healing and the steps along the way to the east from the center are clarity, wisdom and illumination.[17] In the East is the ability to see.[18]

The South is the place of innocence and the inner child.[19] Feelings are emphasized,[20] and the steps from the center are growth, trust and love.[21]

The West provides introspection and space to go within and listen.[22] It is a place of intelligence and acceptance.[23] The steps to the West are experience, introspection and strength.[24]

The North is applied knowledge, a kind of experienced knowing.[25] Wisdom and gratitude rest here.[26] The steps to the North include cleansing, renewal and purity.[27]

Orient & Navigate: The Work of the Shaman: Journeying & Divination

Once again develop a question. Next, find a place where you can walk in the four cardinal directions. It can be a place with which you are intimately familiar or a place entirely new to you. Be sure to take your notebook and a compass.

When you arrive at your chosen destination, establish a center. You may find an open field or a tree that feels right. In some way, mark the spot so you can easily navigate to and from it.

Sit at your center and repeat your question. Silently extend your awareness to the area around you and ask for help in finding answers to your query. When you feel clear and complete with your request for help and the exact wording of your question, write your question in your notebook.

Stand and face the East. Acknowledge the East for the *illumination* it will provide and begin to walk in that direction. Take note of unusual things that you see or that call your attention. When you have written two or three in your notebook, return to your center. Sit and begin to work with the sightings in the same way you did in the prior exercise. Use "Using the idea of ____" and make the question a declarative sentence. Fill in the blank with what you have sighted and work the declarative sentence until you are satisfied with your answer. Upon completion, thank the East for *illumination*.

Repeat this step to the South acknowledging the *growth* that it will provide. Walk, make note of your sightings, return to your center and work with the information. Thank the South for *growth*.

Move to the West acknowledging the *introspection* it will provide. Walk, make note of your sightings, return to your center and work with the information. Thank the West for *introspection*.

Orient & Navigate: The Work of the Shaman: Journeying & Divination

Finish with the North, acknowledging the *wisdom* it will provide. Walk, make note of your sightings, return to your center and work with the information. Thank the North for *wisdom*.

Depending on how many things caught your attention, you will now have 8-12 sentences that answer your question. Spend time in your center contemplating all that you have learned. When you leave your center, thank it for holding you and the work you have completed. Extend once again to all around you and express gratitude.

Exercise #2: Walking the Compass
Date:
Your Question:

East (*illumination*)
1.
Thoughts & Metaphoric Connections:

Using the idea of _____,

2.
Thoughts & Metaphoric Connections:

Using the idea of _____,

3.
Thoughts & Metaphoric Connections:

Using the idea of _____,

Orient & Navigate: The Work of the Shaman: Journeying & Divination

South (*growth*)

1.

Thoughts & Metaphoric Connections:

Using the idea of _____,

2.

Thoughts & Metaphoric Connections:

Using the idea of _____,

3.

Thoughts & Metaphoric Connections:

Using the idea of _____,

West (*introspection*)

1.

Thoughts & Metaphoric Connections:

Using the idea of _____,

2.

Thoughts & Metaphoric Connections:

Orient & Navigate: The Work of the Shaman: Journeying & Divination

Using the idea of _____,

3.
Thoughts & Metaphoric Connections:

Using the idea of _____,

North (*wisdom*)
1.
Thoughts & Metaphoric Connections:

Using the idea of _____,

2.
Thoughts & Metaphoric Connections:

Using the idea of _____,

3.
Thoughts & Metaphoric Connections:

Using the idea of _____,

Orient & Navigate: The Work of the Shaman: Journeying & Divination

Exercise #3: Sitting Observations

This exercise allows the clues to find you. Once again, determine your question and go to a favorite place outside. Walk for several minutes acclimating to the place, and when you are ready look for a spot to sit, a spot that draws you to it. Settle yourself and take note of the direction you will call 'forward.'

Begin by facing one of the six directions established by your body in space—forward, behind, left, right, up and down. It doesn't matter which one. In this exercise you will not be using the cardinal directions; your orientation to the space comes with you as 'center' pulling answers to you versus actively 'walking out' to the answers in particular directions.

For this exercise, you will be exploring your own metaphors as they relate to your body. Forward, or before you, may relate to a sense of future or goal. Behind you may relate to the past—something to leave behind or something that supports your moving ahead. Left and right may have something to do with a surprise (coming in from left field) or following rules (doing it right). Up may be guidance from the Divine. Down may be nurturing from Mother Earth. Explore your own associations with each direction. *Or*, each of the directions is simply an avenue from which information approaches you and there is no apparent metaphoric association. The purpose here is to extend and expand your thoughts about your orientation in space, in this place, by using your body rather than a compass.

Softly look around and see if anything catches your attention. It may be a sound, a scent, a flutter of movement, a bright color, an animal, a plant. Take your time with this. Get accustomed to the wind. You will want to select something that really attracts you. Once you have done this in one direction, repeat it for the other directions. Then, for up and for down. You will have six noteworthy

Orient & Navigate: The Work of the Shaman: Journeying & Divination

items in your journal. If you wish, you may begin the process of seeing how each provides an answer to your question.

Exercise #3: Sitting Observations
Date:
Your Question:

1. Before Me:
Thoughts & Metaphoric Connections:

Using the idea of _____,

2. Behind Me:
Thoughts & Metaphoric Connections:

Using the idea of _____,

3. To My Right:
Thoughts & Metaphoric Connections:

Using the idea of _____,

4. To My Left:
Thoughts & Metaphoric Connections:

Using the idea of _____,

Orient & Navigate: The Work of the Shaman: Journeying & Divination

5. Above Me:
Thoughts & Metaphoric Connections:

Using the idea of _____,

6. Beneath Me:
Thoughts & Metaphoric Connections:

Using the idea of _____,

 The seventh direction is the center—the space and place you physically, mentally and spiritually occupy. You may wish to turn your attention inward to see if an answer rises up from within. This may be a seventh answer.

Orient & Navigate: The Work of the Shaman: Journeying & Divination

Exercise #4: Sensing the Story

This exercise was something my Upper World Teacher suggested I do to practice listening to the landscape. He suggested that I go out to water and listen to its stories. Although it's not strictly a divination exercise, it is a way to practice listening. Answers can come to us through a process, as in Exercises 1 through 3, or they can come to us directly, rather like dictation.

Once again, find a place in nature where you feel safe and comfortable. Sit with your notebook and settle into the place. Notice what surrounds you. When you are ready, pick something there—a tree, a stream, a plant—from which you will take dictation. Reach out to the being, and politely ask it to converse with you. Then open up to hearing what it says. Review Exercise #4: Heart Sensing in Chapter 5 for a little help with this.

This exercise takes patience above all else. And it takes letting go of some notions about who and what can 'talk' to us. But by slowing down and knowing that all things can communicate, you will eventually have a sense of interaction. It may take several attempts to experience this, so keep at it. Once you are able to connect, honor that connection and listen well. Notice the qualitative similarities and differences of the communication as compared to routine human talk. Not only is the message a bit of knowledge, but so is the means.

Orient & Navigate: The Work of the Shaman: Journeying & Divination

 Exercise #4: Sensing the Story

Date:

Who I am listening to:

The dictation: (may come as words, phrases, images, thoughts… open to all kinds of sensations! Write everything down even if you think you are making it up. You can let your analytical mind play later.)

7 Into the Picture

Locate a [stone] monument or site on a map. Drive for hours in a car, and attempt to arrive as close as possible to the place... and you are there... the result is inevitably disappointing... A monument [or site] encountered in the course of a walk between places is an altogether different matter. Approaching it slowly, from different directions, and anticipating arriving, it is possible to observe in a much more subtle manner...
—Christopher Tilley, *A Phenomenology of Landscape*[1]

We can thank the Dutch for the word 'landscape' in our vocabulary. It comes to us from *landschap* and originally was known as 'landskip'. The concept of landscape was initially construed through the artist's eye, since it reminded a viewer of something that could be painted.[2] To use the word 'picturesque' when talking about landforms and pretty places further highlights this mental framework where rural scenery is likened to a picture.

When working shamanically with landscapes via journey or divination, it is important to keep in mind that we are combining this artistic sense of landscape as a fixed representation with a body of ongoing growing and lived experience. Our adventures into and with landscapes are meant to be expansive and cumulative. This ultimately produces relationships for us with distinct locales wherein certain spirits are met and activities conducted.

Landscape as art can be a delightful point of departure for shamanic exploration into a particular feature. The notion that one can 'enter a picture' has precedence in the art world. Nicholas Green in writing about ways to look at landscape cites an art reviewer of the late 1830s who, in an article, invited his readers to "step inside the picture, to sit beneath the painted trees, or dive into the limpid blue of the lake."[3] We of the 1900s and 2000s are likewise familiar with this method of travel into landscapes. Walt Disney pulled movie viewers into a non-ordinary world in his production of *Mary Poppins*. As Disney tells it, Mary, her friend Bert, and Mary's charges Jane and Michael Banks jump into a chalk drawing that Bert has created in the park. During their foray into this other world as depicted in the film via animation, the foursome enjoy a range of activities, from merry making on a carousel to romantically sipping tea—all punctuated with human and human-like animal interplay.[4] There are friends to be found inside the world of the chalk drawing!

While at the surface one might assume that jumping into the drawing was for the amusement of Jane and Michael, I think Mary's intention was to expand the children's limited perception of the world and open their hearts to people and beings outside of their narrow existence in the nursery. The woman in the film who sits on the cathedral steps feeding the birds plants the seed of compassion, as does the presence of Bert and the chimney sweeps. We, too, wish to expand our view and open our hearts. This is the intention that guides us and encourages us to develop a familiarity with the features and move beyond the spectatorship suggested in the article from the 1830s. We don't want to simply sit by the lake. Our task is to actively engage the landscape in an intimate way. We begin by selecting a stage upon which the action is to take place—that is, a particular landscape—and we program ourselves for a particular journey. This notion of programming has been used extensively in dream work and sleep studies as a way to 'stack the deck' in favor of having an experience. Our intention guides our work and upon entering via an image, landscape becomes a field of praxis.

Once a landscape is selected, the way to enter into a drawing or photograph is to put as much awareness as possible into the picture.

In shamanic terms, you take a journey. From the chair or floor (if you are lying down), close your eyes, listen to the monotonous percussion of the drum and step with as much of your awareness as possible into the picture. The 1933 film *Alice in Wonderland* shows a very brave Charlotte Henry as Alice stepping over and through the frame of a mirror to arrive in another world.[5] We can do the same.

At first, our experience may be vague or hazy. Yet, with repeated visits, resolution will improve. Once you have established your place in the picture, it may help to ask yourself: What do I hear?; What do I smell?; What do I see?; What do I feel?; What do I taste?; What do I know? Move through the environment and sense what is beyond the edges. For example, take a walk and find out what is over the hill, behind the tree or under the water. It is common during the initial phases of the survey to have awareness of your physical body in the chair or on the floor, as well as your journeying body in the picture. Much like a radio, you are tuning into two worlds and you are able to pick up both. On the journey shift your focus to non-ordinary reality as much as you can.

Your first journey into a picture may not seem to yield much. As with most endeavors, it is repetition that will lead to mastery. With repeated journeys into a specific landscape picture, you will gain familiarity and the knowledge of what exists beyond the ordinary reality frame. Observe the plants; see what animals or people are living there; check out the rocks; take note of the temperature and humidity. All of these things represent intelligence and have the potential for informing.

After you have become acquainted with a particular landscape, you may wish to intentionally visit it with a question. Divination in its broadest sense is the retrieval of hidden knowledge through spiritual or supernatural means. Upon entering the landscape, present your question and see what happens. It has been said that everything that occurs on a journey after you ask your question is part of the answer. When you return from your journey, record your experience. The answer to your question may be very obvious. The prairie may have whispered in words to you. The river may have shown you a scene that answers your question. In facing the salt flat, you may have gotten what Robert Monroe has called a "thought-ball," a complete package of knowing.[6] Or you may have experienced symbols that can be understood by going through the process learned in the divination exercises of Chapter 6. You even may have met an animal or plant friend who shared some good advice.

Using an image is a way to focus on a specific landscape and carry your intention to communicate with it into non-ordinary reality. This can be expanded to include contact with specific intelligence within a landscape. Earlier the Makers, Keepers and Guardians were introduced. Now, as you are at the threshold, perched to enter landscapes, further mention of these beings is warranted. If for example, you wish to contact the intelligence of the Fire Maker in a landscape, you can enter the landscape and make your intention known—politely. These beings are powerful and respect is the watchword during your explorations. The Fire Maker may immediately come forward and communicate with you in a readily accessible way. However, because the Makers' way of being is outside our human frame of reference, it may become necessary to employ an identifying technique to validate and detect an encounter with a Maker. If you are not getting any recognizable response to your request for contact, look for a symbol of the Maker you seek. The symbol can be of your own design, a random symbol, or you can use the following that have been well established historically.

Astrology has given us fire, earth, air and water in order as represented below.[7]

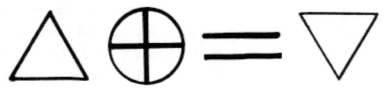

Alchemy uses the following symbols, left to right, the elements of fire, air, earth and water.[8, 9]

Recalling that the Makers are beings of movement and action, you may choose the wavy lines for flowing water[10] and the bisected triangle for burning fire.[11]

If I am seeking the Fire Maker, I look for the symbol for burning fire. Although the symbol you use is less important than your intention to find it within the landscape, selecting one that makes sense to you may assist you in these explorations. Once you find the symbol in the landscape, go to it and treat it as a doorway to the Maker. Announce to the Maker your desire to learn and wait for the door of communication to open to you.

These same instructions apply to the search for Guardians and Keepers. Step into the landscape and state your intention to contact the Guardian of a landform, the being overseeing all of a category of landscape, for example all tidal pools, or the Keeper who looks after a particular landform, for example, a specific tidal pool. Understand that these beings will make themselves known in a way that you can comprehend—a way which may or may not be their ultimate identity. They are doing what they can to speak to you in the vocabulary of your experience. Learning to recognize these beings and how to communicate with them will be the result of the relationships you build through repeated visits. Once again, if you have difficulty in recognizing them within the landscape, assign a symbol that makes sense to you and seek it on your journey.

You will have the opportunity to practice making connections with Keepers, Makers and Guardians in the following Orient & Navigate by using the journey or Alice's mode of stepping into the picture. These are ways to access information and stretch your awareness beyond the capacity you normally use in your day-to-day encounters with the world. The exercises require you to slow down and shift your focus from thoughts of the past and plans for the future. Awareness becomes a practice of immediacy.

Orient & Navigate: Into the Picture

Exercise #1: Contemplating Landscape

Select a familiar landscape, perhaps the space that you drive through on the way to work or a special place where you have vacationed.

1. Consider all the possible components of the landscape: geophysical feature, flora, fauna, Keeper, Maker and Guardian. What's most obvious to you? What takes some time for you to notice? What might you be missing? How can you discover it?

2. Consider how the landscape and your life are related.

3. Consider what it took for the landscape to exist.

4. Pretend you are the landscape. This is shamanic merging. Imagine what you might feel and get the sense of yourself as the landscape as you go through your day. How does the landscape affect your perception of your day? Yourself?

5. How do you relate to the landscape? Rush through it? Stop and enjoy it? Resent it as a barrier to a destination?

6. What does the landscape have to tell you about where you're currently living or how you're currently living?

7. Assign or create a place name for the landscape. What does this name tell you about the associations and thoughts that you already have surrounding it?

8. Consider the idea of boundaries within the landscape. Where does it begin? End? Where is there a betwixt-and-between place?

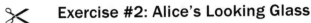

Orient & Navigate: Into the Picture

Exercise #2: Alice's Looking Glass

Step into a landscape as Alice stepped into the looking glass. Use a drawing you have made, a photo or a painting. It doesn't have to be a place that you have been or that you already know. Close your eyes and feel your awareness move into the landscape. You may do this with your imagination or, if you know how to journey, using that method. Choose one of the following suggestions. It is best to take only one suggestion at a time and allow the experience to fully unfold rather than try all the questions at once.

1. Look for a Guardian, the one who oversees all of this type of landscape, for example, the Guardian of all marshes. Politely ask for a lesson from the landscape according to this being.

2. Enter the landscape with the eyes of a child. What do you see that excites you, makes you feel warm and fuzzy or warns you (this is an expanded understanding of biophilia)?

3. Pretend to see the spirits of the landscape. What do they look like?

4. Ask the landscape what you and it share, how you both are the same.

5. Sit in the environment of the landscape and see what happens.

6. Ask the landscape, what do I need to know today?

7. Find a helper (animal, plant, mineral or spirit) from the landscape and ask it a question.

Orient & Navigate: Into the Picture

Exercise #3: Middle World Exploration

Take a Middle World journey to an actual feature or place. For example, journey to Lake Michigan or another lake of your choice if you select 'lake' as your landscape feature. (If you don't know how to journey, imagine going to an actual place.)

1. Look for the Keeper, the one who tends this specific landscape. Ask for the lesson from the landscape according to this being.

2. Enter the landscape with the eyes of a child. What do you see?

3. Practice looking for spirits in the landscape.

4. Ask the landscape what it represents to you.

5. Sit in the environment and see what happens.

6. Ask what you need to know in the moment.

7. Find a helper in the landscape and ask it a question.

Orient & Navigate: Into the Picture

For the next three exercises, it may be useful to pick one place and work with it. As you do so, you will be building knowledge of the qualitative differences between ordinary and non-ordinary reality as well as the variation between Guardians (overarching form), Makers (verbs of creation), and Keepers (tenders of specific, individual expressions of form and movement).

Exercise #4: Connecting with a Maker

To connect with a Maker, step into a landscape that you know, using either Alice's looking glass method or through a Middle World journey. Ask to meet the Maker involved in its creation. To help you find a place to meet, use your shamanic vision to locate one of the symbols of the Makers and place yourself on or by it. Enter the landscape with the intention that the appearance of the symbol in the landscape indicates that the Maker is open to your approach. You may have to repeat this several times before you meet a Maker.

Place Visited:

Means Accessed (Middle World Journey, Alice's Looking Glass):

Date:

Maker Sought:

Marker Used:

Journey Notes:

Orient & Navigate: Into the Picture

Exercise #5: Visiting the Keeper of a Landscape

Visit a specific landscape feature's spirit in the Upper or Lower World. For example, journey to find the spirit of Mount Everest. This is a visit to a specific mountain spirit in non-ordinary reality—the spirit of a Keeper. If you first visit the spirit in the Lower World, take a subsequent journey to the Upper World for a visit. Notice if there is a difference between your experience of it in the Upper and/or Lower World and in the ordinary reality and non-ordinary reality of the Middle World. If different, how? What does this tell you?

Place Visited (ordinary reality):

Otherworld Accessed (Lower World, Upper World):

Date:

Journey Notes:

Exercise #6: Visiting the Guardian of a Landscape

Visit a specific landscape feature's form spirit in the Upper or Lower World. For example, journey to find the spirit of all mountains. If you first visit the spirit in the Lower World, take a subsequent journey to the Upper World for a visit. Notice if there is a difference between your experience of it in the Upper and/or Lower World. If different, how? What does this tell you?

Form Visited (ordinary reality):

Otherworld Accessed (Lower World, Upper World):

Date:

Journey Notes:

Orient & Navigate: Into the Picture

Exercise #7: Landscape Art

Many of us are fortunate to have art and art museums within easy access. Even if that isn't the case, the internet is an art museum at a click. As you work and expand your level of intimacy with landscapes, you may be drawn to the paintings of landscape artists.

As you become acquainted with paintings and photographs, you may want to collect postcards (at art museum gift shops) or other images of them and use them as entry ways into landscapes. You can make a deck of postcards, each with a different scene, and use it for a divinatory reading; this is called cartomancy. Pick a card and study it. The way you feel and what you know of that landscape can clue you in to the message of the moment.

Below is a list of paintings and artists. Do you know these? Others? Without the analytical eye of the art critic, but rather with the view from the heart center, what feelings are elicited? Add to the list and highlight your favorites.

Artist	Title of Work	Landscape Represented
Claude Monet	Banks of the Seine	River
Thomas Cole	Falls of the Kaaterskill	Stream
George Catlin	Luxuriant forest on the bank of the Amazon	Tropical Rainforest
Frederick Edwin Church	Rainy Season in the Tropics	Deciduous Monsoon Forest
Frederick Edwin Church	Heart of the Andes	Folded Mountains
Frederick Edwin Church	Cotopaxi	Volcano
Asher B. Durand	In the Woods	Deciduous Forest
Thomas Moran	The Grand Canyon of the Yellowstone	Canyon
John LaFarge	The Last Valley Paradise Rocks	Valley
Mark Conlin	Fiji Barrier Reef	Reef

Orient & Navigate: Into the Picture

Conrad Buff	Pinnacle	Spire
Northern Song or Jin Dynasty	Streams and Mountains without End	Karst
Louis Remy Mignot	Niagara Falls	River, Falls
Jules Dupre	On the Marsh	Marshland
Jean Baptiste Camille Corot	Lake Nemi	Lake
Albert Bierstadt	Emerald Sea	Beach

Your Favorites:

8 The Terra Signs

STEEPING
When you sit in a spot, your energy
becomes saturated with the tone of the place.
Imagine a teabag that had no flavor, color or properties
of its own, but only absorbed the qualities around it.
Let yourself sit until you are done.
—Frederic Lehrman, *The Sacred Landscape*[1]

When we look to landscape, we are not all looking with the same eyes. Each of us has grown up with a unique set of experiences, and the meaning we draw from what we see reflects this uniqueness. Unlike the Australian Aborigines, we haven't been schooled to look at a particular small conical rock and see 'Maggot Power' as reported by Bruce Chatwin in *The Songlines*. We each see our rocks through the screen of different metaphors. This probably becomes most obvious when we examine our reactions to specific landscapes. For some, the idea of 'mountain' connects to climbing and height, perhaps even spiritual attainment. But even this connection diverges. One may further connect climbing to ultimate torture: burning lungs on the way up, aching legs on the way down. Another will connect to the exhilaration of the climb as a way to test one's mettle and prove one's superior fitness. Landscape is a product not only of what we see, but also how we interact with and experience it.

Yet, there are also certain congruencies in the way we view landscape. Similar enculturation may account for this. For English speakers, John Masefield gave us the lonely and alluring sea, complete with gray dawn and wind "like a whetted knife." Coleridge enchanted us with a sacred river running through "caverns measureless to man, down to a sunless sea." Through shared references to the ocean or caverns, for example, we have been impressed with images that fuel our thoughts and imaginations, which in turn become an interpretive filter when we are exposed to a particular landscape.

As Hirsch tells us, "there is no absolute landscape."[2] For those of us using landscape for divination and inspiration, what this means is that we are free from a strict sense of meaning or even our own cultural instruction. Our interaction with landscape is an ongoing process building on accumulated experiences and rooted in our personal perspective. We have not been taught that hills mean 'thus and such.' Though we may share a common frame of reference by virtue of schooling or experience, as individuals our sense of place will be different from each other's. Our memories for the most part are shared in only a limited way by a well-defined group, as we experienced in the writing Orient & Navigate exercise of an Apache-style tale and the listing of Penan-style place names.

As the reader, your idea of 'river' and what it means to you may be very different from my idea of 'river.' What follows is an examination of various landscapes or features using a standard dictionary-style definition as a starting point. Certain aspects of the definition are set in **bold text** to form the seeds of questions for contemplation. This is your invitation to work to expand your personal metaphor, one enriched by your direct, personal experience. In presenting this list, the landscapes are defined in order to provide a clear understanding of the system or mechanism involved in forming them or the flora and fauna living in them—a very technical approach. Deeper understanding will come to each individual in time through contemplation and journeying. Using your journal to answer the questions may also yield insights—in fact, it's strongly recommended. Also, I would suggest highlighting words in the definitions that resonate with you personally. Or find another dictionary definition that captures a certain 'something' for you. Make the definition and description your own; develop your own questions and your personalized sense of the feature.

Up until this moment, the forms of the land and waters have been called features and landscapes. Now, as you shift your understanding and awareness from the ordinary and technical, your relationship with the features and landscapes will shift; they are more appropriately called *terra signs*. They are 'terra' because they are of the Earth. They are 'signs' because they can be read metaphorically with a sense of deeper meaning and far greater significance.

The *terra signs* outlined in the list below are meant to be part of an ongoing interactive process. Several cautions are essential before you begin:

1. When considering a landscape, it may be tempting to think that it must be wilderness, a place uninhabited by humans. Not so.

2. The idea of empty land or *terra nullius* is closely related. There is no empty land; all land is infused with intelligence and consciousness.[3]

3. Landscapes that appear untouched by human hands, pristine, may very well be cultural landscapes created by people. Though touched in that way, they still inform.

4. Words are metaphors. We use them to communicate verbally to each other. Your computer 'mouse' isn't a mammalian mouse. However, the idea of a small mechanical device that scoots along the desk with a tail (cord) leading to a computer is very suggestive of a mammalian mouse and makes the signifier useful. While we search for language to communicate about landscapes, we are somewhat tied to mechanistic language that uses words like 'component' and 'feature' as signifiers. Begin thinking of these as *terra signs*—

they have intelligence and consciousness that we are working to engage. They are alive and exist outside of our interactions, and thus they deserve our respect.

5. Categorization of landscapes is a human tool, not a mandate. It is a lens through which we can explore spiritual relationships and manage them. It helps us to focus as we seek ever-deepening understanding. If the method of organization presented here doesn't serve your purpose, reorganize! This is meant as a starting point.

6. Choosing to work with a *terra sign* is not a one-time event. Relationships with the landscape and the spirits in it are evolving and dynamic; multiple explorations of a single *terra sign* will provide richness that builds over time. Just like friendships, these relationships take work, time and attention.

In selecting features to be represented as *terra signs*, the decision was made to use a mix of physical, geographic, and biome identifiers. Strictly speaking, each physical feature may be made up of multiple biomes, as in the case of a mountain with its base in a rainforest and its peak surrounded by alpine tundra. And similarly, a biome may be found in association with multiple geophysical features. Think of the tall grass prairie in a river valley or sweeping across a plain. The purpose in compiling the list of signs was to provide a degree of focus while at the same time avoiding strict limitation. Mixing geophysical features with biomes was the best tactic for achieving that goal. And while attempting neutrality through the use of technical definitions, my relationship and memory of landscape colors the questions. Use your discernment. The **seed words** I have chosen to highlight in **bold type** were selected according to my point of view, because they, to me, are defining or fundamental descriptors of a given *terra sign*.

The Individual Terra Signs[4]

It is one of the imperatives of nature that nothing remains constant. Climates change. Mountains erode. Rivers embark on new courses. Deserts and forests march and retreat. Ice flows melt. Seas rise. Volcanoes alter the landscape, their debris darkening the sky and dimming the sun. Tidal waves and storms chew relentlessly at the shores. Islands rise and vanish. The mighty plates undergrinding the continents are themselves ever in motion. The grain of sand was once a boulder. A new Atlantis may even now be imperceptibly vanishing into the deep, or an old submerged and vanquished mountain may be preparing to reassert itself.
—William Longgood, *The Queen Must Die*[5]

Freshwater

Freshwater is essential for human life. The average human is comprised of about 65% water. Of the 340 million cubic miles of water on Earth, less than 3% of it is fresh. Although found in the atmosphere (0.001%) as well as lakes and rivers (0.01%), the two greatest reservoirs of freshwater are the polar ice caps, including glaciers, and the ground (2.1% and 0.6%, respectively). Freshwater is very precious.

The water cycle circulates freshwater on the face of the Earth. Water in the air condenses and forms clouds. Clouds cool and it precipitates. **Water collects and moves, runs off or is stored. It returns to the air via evaporation and transpiration.**

Lake

Related Landscape Terms: loch, tarn, maar, kettle lake, lough, oxbow lake, billabong

One of the **storehouses** of liquid freshwater is lakes. Lakes are inland bodies of **still** water and form when there is some **barrier** to normal drainage or run off. Some are the result of faults such as Lake

Baikal that occupies a graben. Others like Lake Chad are formed when stresses upon the Earth's crust make subsidence basins that fill with water. Still others are the products of past volcanic activity such as Crater Lake, which formed when water filled a volcanic crater. When volcanoes explode so violently and no collapsed cone or caldera remains, a lake may form in the resulting basin. This is called a maar and the Laacher See is an example. When glaciers carve basins at the heads of valleys and these fill with water, tarns are formed. Kettle lakes also form as a result of glaciation; depressions, left when a glacier recedes, fill with melting water.

Lake Questions:
1. What disturbs your peace? What can you do to find stillness?
2. What are you collecting around you? Friends? Experiences?
3. What feeds or supports you? What do you support?
4. What are the circumstances under which you block the flow in your life?

Examples: Lake Baikal, Siberia (the oldest and deepest); Lake Titicaca, South America (highest navigable and largest freshwater lake in South America); Lake Superior, North America (the largest freshwater lake by surface area and second largest by volume); Lake Chad, Africa; Crater Lake, Oregon (deepest lake in US); Laacher See

Pond

Related Landscape Terms: prairie pothole, kettle lake, kettle hole, pool, lochan

Ponds, like lakes, are also **storehouses** of still freshwater, but on a much **smaller** scale. Some say that a body of water is a pond if a person can walk across it without submerging or if sunlight can reach the bottom. The classification is somewhat subjective. There are more than 2 million ponds in North America and most began as hollows carved by glaciers; oxbow lakes cut off from streams; and depressions made in soluble rock. Ponds generally have a shorter life cycle, only hundreds of years, compared to that of lakes. They begin with water **filling** the depressions through rain or springs and eventually become filled with microscopic life carried in by rain and wind. More complex plant and animal life arrives via waterfowl. **Over time** silt and organic materials fill the pond and provide a roothold for woody plants and the water level lowers. The pond then becomes a marsh. Glacial ponds in northern grasslands are often called prairie potholes.

Pond Questions:

1. What interferes with your spiritual life?
2. How can you think or dream bigger? In what ways are you limiting yourself?
3. How are your dreams evolving?
4. What are you doing to bring life to your dreams?

Examples: Walden Pond; Jamaica Pond; Ell Pond, New England (kettle hole); Lake Ronkonkoma, Long Island (kettle hole)

Wetlands

Related Landscape Terms: bog, muskeg, moor, mangrove swamp, mangal, marsh, swamp, carr, fen, mire, bayou, slough

There are three basic areas of **waterlogged** vegetation known as wetlands: marsh, swamp and bog. These areas are distinguished mostly by the vegetation **growing** in them. The marsh is covered with grasses, the swamp with trees and the bog with grasses and sphagnum moss often forming floating beds of vegetation. The Florida Everglades is an excellent and huge example of a marsh, as is Bass Harbor, Maine. Bald Cypress Bayou is an example of a swamp, while the New Jersey Pine Barrens is a bog. Bogs are often further classified: peatland or mire, where vegetation is being produced **faster than it decomposes** and forms peat, a brown organic material; a bog, filled with grasses and rain water; and a fen, filled with sedges and ground water. Other wetland terms include blanket mire, muskegs and moors. The primary reason for the formation of these wetlands is a **blockage** to the flow of freshwater.

Wetlands Questions:
1. Is there something stagnant or decaying in your life?
2. Are you bogged down in any area of your life?
3. Where do you feel swamped?
4. Where do you find richness and growth?

Examples: Florida Everglades (marsh); New Jersey Pine Barrens (bog); Bald Cypress Bayou (swamp); Pantanal, Brazil (world's largest wetlands)

River

Related Landscape Terms: source, channel, mouth, rapids, waterfall, cataract, delta, pothole, eddy, estuary

Water that **flows** in one **direction** characterizes a river. It is a system of freshwater flow that begins at a source, follows a **channel** and dumps into the ocean through a mouth. The channel makes its way across a floodplain in any of the following patterns: straight, like parts of the Columbia and Colorado Rivers; meandering, like parts of the Mississippi; braided, like the Platte; or anastomosing (a network of many twisting branches), like the Amazon. At times various channels of the river get cut off, forming oxbow lakes or billabongs. There are times the water moves quickly due to a **change in grade** and there are rapids, waterfalls, cascades or cataracts. And, often, at the river's mouth there are deposits of silt that form a delta in various patterns: arcuate, like the Nile Delta; cuspate, like the delta of the Niger River; and bird's foot, like the Mississippi. When the freshwater of a river encounters and mixes with sea water, the result is an estuary: a vertically homogenous estuary, partially mixed estuary or salt wedge estuary depending on tides and currents.

River Questions:
1. How can you relate the system of the river—from source to delta—to the goals you set and the way you go about achieving them?

2. How can you characterize your communication style—straight, braided, meandering, anastomosing? Does this pattern serve you? What would you prefer?

3. Do you go with the flow or fight the flow? Do you rush headlong into things and end up unsupported and out of control, or do you get caught up in situations that hurdle you around and around getting nowhere?

4. What's your relationship to time?

Examples: Amazon River, South America (largest); Nile, Egypt (longest); De La Plata, South America (widest); Ganges, India; Mississippi River Delta, United States (largest US delta); Mississippi-Missouri River System, United States (longest in US); Yangtze, China; Yosemite Falls, California (tallest US waterfall); Niagara Falls, NY; Angel Falls, Venezuela (highest falls); Iguacu Falls, Argentina & Paraguay (widest falls); Okavango Delta, Kalahari (largest inland delta)

Stream

Related Landscape Terms: spring, rill, brook, creek, tributary, run, fork, beck, burn, kill, riffle, branch

Like rivers, streams are **moving** freshwater. These features flow faster than rivers and are much closer to the **source**. Streams form tributaries—water flowing into and **contributing** to much larger courses. When streams meet, it is at a **confluence**. Other names applied to the tributaries of rivers in order of magnitude include: spring, rill, brook, creek and stream.

Stream Questions:
1. What do you contribute to in a positive way? In a negative way? Financially, emotionally, physically?
2. How would you characterize your relationship to your source of well-being and life?
3. What characterizes the way you come together with others? Conflict? Cooperation? Negotiation? Consensus building?
4. What are your abilities to synthesize ideas?

Examples: Peekskill, New York; Yellow River, Indiana

Glacier

Related Landscape Terms: cirque, arête, horn, firn, crevasse, esker, moraine, drumlin, fjord, iceberg, ice field, kame, névé

Glaciers are masses of freshwater **locked** into ice that move downhill under the **force** of their own **weight**. At the uppermost end of a glacier there are easily recognizable formations: the cirque or steep-sided semi-circular basin; the arête, a sharp ridge; the horn, a pyramidal peak formed when adjacent cirques cut an arête; and the firn or compacted snow field putting weight and pressure on the system. Like a river, the glacier flows downward and leaves **deposits** in the form of eskers, moraines, kames and drumlins. When the ice **cracks** a crevasse is formed. When deep valleys formed by the glacier's **cutting** become flooded when the ice melts, fjords are formed. And, should a piece of the glacier **break** off and slide into the ocean, an iceberg is the result.

Glacier Questions:
1. Do you grasp for control, or do you let things happen under their own momentum?
2. Under what circumstances will you crack?

3. What does it take for you to warm up to people? Is there a façade that has to melt? What is hidden underneath? How much of yourself do you share with others?

4. What is left in your wake as you move through your life?

Examples: Hubbard Glacier, Alaska (alpine glacier); Malaspina Glacier, Alaska (piedmont glacier); Bering Glacier, Alaska (largest in US); Killary Harbour, Ireland (Ireland's only major fjord); Baltoro Glacier, Pakistan (largest glacier outside of a polar region)

Forests and Woodlands

Forests are plant **communities** made up of trees. Trees can be coniferous or deciduous, each having different strategies for survival and each **supporting** different kinds of life. Conifers are among the **oldest** plants on Earth; they have softer wood than their deciduous relatives, grow **needles** and do well in harsh environs. Deciduous or hardwoods have **broad leaves** and a decided photosynthetic advantage, yet cannot extend into more severe climes. Together, conifers and deciduous trees make up the forests which cover about one third of Earth's land area and account for over two thirds of the leaf area of land plants.

A distinction is made between forest and woodland. In the forest, the canopy is solid. Tree leaves meet and entwine so that little **light** reaches the forest floor. Woodland is not as **compact**. Trees have space and the canopy is more **open,** allowing for light to filter through to the ground.

Tropical forests are found within the latitudes of 23.5 degrees north and 23.5 degrees south and are characterized by two seasons—rainy or wet. Temperate forests lie between 23.5 and 66.5 degrees in the north and 23.5 and 66.5 degrees in the south, have **four distinct seasons**, and a growing season of 140-200 days. Boreal forests are defined by their location between 50 and 60 degrees latitude and their two **seasons**: a short, moist, moderately warm summer and a long, cold, dry winter.

Tropical Rainforest
Related Landscape Terms: jungle

Covering less than 7% of the Earth's surface and home to 50-90% of the Earth's animal species, the tropical rainforest is the premier forest for the number and **diversity** of species represented. There is little or no dry season. Most of the trees and plants have broad evergreen leaves; orchids, bromeliads, lianas, ferns, mosses and palms are represented. Birds, monkeys, snakes and lizards populate the understory. **Microhabitats**—small, specialized environments—abound and play a role in the **creation** of new species.

Tropical Rainforest Questions:
1. Do you express all the aspects of yourself?
2. What adds richness to your life?
3. What strategies do you have for relating to diversity—in yourself, your community, and the world?
4. How do you bring forth the primal?

Examples: Buru Rainforests, Indonesia; Andaman Islands, India; Amazon Rainforest, Amazon Basin, South America

Deciduous Monsoon Forest
Related Landscape Terms: jungle

All trees in this forest are deciduous. There are distinct **seasons** of **wet** and dry; during the dry season, the trees, such as teak and ebony, lose their leaves to conserve water. Most of the trees and plants have broad evergreen leaves and animal life includes monkeys, large cats, rodents, parrots and various ground birds.

Deciduous Monsoon Forest Questions:
1. What are your emotional seasons?

2. How do you express sorrow in your life?

3. What moves you from one emotional state to another?

4. How do you cope when life feels dry and boring?

Examples: East Deccan forests, India; southeastern Indochina; Pacific coastal regions of Mexico and Central America

Tropical Scrub

Related Landscape Terms: tomillares, macchia, maquis, phrygana, brigalow, strandveld, chaparral, scrubland, heathland, matorral, batha, garrigue, kwongan

These woodlands border other types of forests and are regions of **slight** rainfall or **poor** soil. Things struggle to grow and often are stunted. They are called by many names: tomillares in the Spanish and Mediterranean climate; macchia or maquis in Mediterranean countries; strandveld or fynbos in South Africa; maquis in other parts of Africa; phrygana in the Balkans; brigalow shrub, sand-heath or kwongan in South Australia; batha in Israel; garrigue in France; matorral in central Chile. Often called chaparral in North America, these areas are characterized by **small** evergreens and **scrub** oak. These shrubs are often found intermixed with grasses and herbs.

Tropical Scrub Questions:

1. What talents or skills do you have that are underdeveloped?

2. What makes you a survivor?

3. How do you survive in harsh times?

4. What are your toughest most overlooked facets?

Examples: Santa Ynez Mountains, Santa Barbara, California; Western Cape, South Africa; Matorral, central Chile

Temperate Deciduous Forest

The temperate forests cover **vast ranges** of climate zones. In North America various species of trees have regions of proliferation. In the cooler north are the sugar maples, birches and beeches. Moving southward into warmer areas there is a mix of oak and hickory. Of course, there are some conifers **mixed** in: hemlock to the north and various pines—loblolly, short- and long- leaf pines and slash pines—to the south.

Temperate Deciduous Forest Questions:

1. How do you honor your cycles of expansion and contraction? Your creativity?
2. What methods do you use to get along with others?
3. What way do you express moderation in your life?
4. How do you keep from getting lost in the crowd?

Examples: Allegheny Highlands, Atlantic coast to edge of Great Plains; Northern Deciduous, New England; Southern New England to East Central Texas, Piedmont

Temperate Rainforest

Mild ocean winds and plenty of moisture provide for these North American forests and their most spectacular residents, the **ancient** redwoods. Also in residence are hemlocks, western red cedars, Sitka spruces, and Douglas firs, many of which are very old.

Temperate Rainforest Questions:

1. Where do you seek ancestral knowledge?
2. How do you connect with and honor your ancestors?
3. What are you doing to pave the way for your descendents?
4. Do you live in a manner that allows for succeeding generations?

Examples: Hoh Rainforest, Pacific Northwest; Olympic National Park, Washington

Temperate Evergreen Forest

The subtropics around Florida and the Caribbean are some of the best-developed **evergreen** forests. Populating these forests are live oaks, magnolias, palms and bromeliads. Gumbo-limbos and mangroves are also present, although mangroves are often associated with **swamps**.

Temperate Evergreen Forest Questions:

1. How do you move beyond apathy and lethargy?
2. How do you strike a balance between activity and inactivity?
3. What inspires or motivates you?
4. What is your approach to risk-taking? Do you play it too safe? Do you throw caution to the wind?

Examples: Gulf of Mexico coast; southern Atlantic coast; southern Florida

Northern Coniferous Forest

Related Landscape Terms: boreal forest, taiga

Growing in increasingly cooler regions, these boreal forests are made up of spruce, fir and tamarack trees with a few **hardy** birches and aspens in the more northerly regions and pine, larch, and hemlock farther south. Landscape features commonly associated with these forests are mountains, lakes, rivers and bogs. In Russia, they are known as the taiga. These forests are home to herbivorous mammals, migrating birds, bears, lynxes, wolves, raccoons, weasels and raptors, to name a few. There are two **seasons**: a short, moist, moderately warm summer and a long, cold, dry, **dark** winter.

Northern Coniferous Forest Questions:

1. What do you do to rest?

2. Is there a pattern or cycle to your expenditure of energy?
3. How would you characterize yourself: 'needler' or 'needled'? What advantage might there be in shifting one to the other?
4. How do you find light in the darkness?

Examples: northern Northeast and Canadian Maritimes to British Columbia and Alaska; Glacier National Park, Montana

Plains and Grasslands

Plains are extensive areas of flat or slightly rolling land. The way they were formed determines the type: alluvial-, coastal-, or floodplains. In temperate regions, plains are distinctive for grasses and a marked absence of trees. In these regions they are called grasslands.

In North America tracts of grassland are often called prairies. Ninety percent of a prairie lies **below** the surface of the ground as part of an enormous **root system,** much of which can live 50 years or more, while the surface above may green only occasionally after a bit of rain. Grasses hold soil erosion and moisture loss in check and are drought resistant. North America's largest natural **community** is grassland. Various names have been associated with grasslands, including the veldt of South Africa, the puszta of Hungary, the pampas and paramos of Argentina and Uruguay, the steppes of the former Soviet Union and the llanos of Columbia and Venezuela.

Prairie

Prairies are classified as short, mixed or tall grass depending on the height of the grasses growing across them. Height is dependent upon rainfall—the greater the rainfall, the higher the grass. When rainfall is particularly low, prairie grasses grow to less than two feet high. Comprising these tracts of short grass prairie are plants with smaller tops and deep roots that can store water under dry conditions. West Kansas's short grass prairie is home to buffalo grass, blue grama and little bluestem.

As rain becomes a bit more plentiful, grasses grow higher—between two and four feet. Lostwood Wildlife Refuge in North Dakota is an example of a mixed grass prairie where little bluestem grass, western wheat grass, pasque flower and golden ragwort can be found. This prairie is a transitional zone where a mix of species from tall and short grass prairies mingle.

The tall grass prairies have the most rain and are home to vegetation in excess of four feet in height. They roll out from the vestiges of the eastern deciduous forests from South Bend, Indiana through Iowa and into Nebraska. Among the species found in Osage Hills, Oklahoma, an example of a tall grass prairie, are bluestem, yellow Indian grass, coneflower, rattlesnake master, goldenrod and the western prairie fringed orchid, which grows up to eight feet tall. Other tall grass prairies are Sheyenne National Grasslands in North Dakota and Tall Grass Prairie Preserve near Pawhuska, Oklahoma.

Prairie Questions:

1. What is your sense of community?
2. What do you do to distinguish yourself from the crowd?
3. How do you come back from burn out?
4. Do you ever go underground as a way to rest and regroup?

Examples: Osage Hills, OK (tall grass); Sheyenne National Grasslands & Little Missouri, ND (tall grass); Lostwood Wildlife Refuge, ND (mixed grass); West Kansas (short grass)

Alluvial & Flood Plains

A level tract of land formed from **suspended** sand and silt carried by a river is an alluvial plain. If the sand and silt, called alluvium, is **deposited** at the mouth of the river, it forms a delta. If it is deposited at a point where the river channel widens, it is called an alluvial fan. And, when a river bursts its banks and deposits the alluvium on the adjacent land, it is contributing sediment to the floodplain. Land inundated or created by alluvium is some of the most **fertile**.

Alluvial & Flood Plains Questions:

1. What do you carry with you as you move through life?
2. How do you contribute to the lives of others?
3. How can you turn destruction into creativity?
4. Where is the fertile ground in your life? How do you tend this ground?

   Examples: Nile River Valley; Mississippi River Valley

Coastal Plain

Related Landscape Terms: machair, machar

Flat land that borders a seacoast and is a **transition** area to the nearest elevated ground is a coastal plain. This expanse may be formed through the deposition of sediment carried by rivers, **erosion** of land by the sea, **uplift** of the Earth's crust or emergence of the continental shelf due to a drop in sea level.

Coastal Plain Questions:

1. What does it mean to you to be or feel flat?
2. How do you cope when you are between two extremes?
3. How do you react to the actions of those around you who attempt to diminish you?
4. How do you react to the actions of those around you who are attempting to elevate you?

   Examples: Berneray, Outer Hebrides (machair); Atlantic coastal plain; Israeli coastal plain

Arctic Tundra

Related Landscape Terms: tundra, páramo

This **treeless** plain is found in arctic and subarctic regions north of the coniferous forests, where it is **frozen** most of the year. In these far northern regions there is a mixture of low-growing sedges, grasses, mosses, and lichens that have a very **brief** growing season in summer when the topsoil **thaws**. Caribou, musk ox, lemmings and polar bears are representatives of the few faunal species able to live in this region.

Arctic Tundra Questions:

1. What part of your life is rigid?
2. In what ways might you benefit from a clear vista or perspective?
3. When have you been locked into a point of view? About what?
4. What would it take for you to lessen the rigidity in your life?

Examples: Alaska; northern Canada; Lapland, Russia

Savanna

Related Landscape Terms: llanos, campos, cerrados

Although sometimes classified as a forest, the savanna is predominantly populated by grasses and forbs, small broad-leaved plants that grow with grasses. This grassland has only a scattering of thorny trees and drought resistant undergrowth, since the lack of rain in the marked dry season prevents the growth of forests. The most extensive savannas are found in Africa where **seasonal migrations** of magnitude play out their drama.

Savanna Questions:

1. Where do you seek movement in your life?
2. How do you quench your thirst for life?

3. What do you do to tune into your physical, emotional and spiritual prompting?
4. How do you work with the cycles of plenty and scarcity in your life?

Examples: Serengeti, Africa

Steppe

Steppes are **vast** grass plains with hot summers and cold winters. They have short grasses, usually no greater than a foot in height, and receive less rain than the short grass prairies. Plants include blue grama and buffalo grass as well as cacti, sagebrush and speargrass. Usually the term steppe is applied to grasslands in Eurasia, although North America has its share of steppe areas.

Steppe Questions:

1. What is your strategy for managing extremes?
2. How do you collect and bolster your resources?
3. Can you face being alone?
4. Do you always need to be connected to others via texting, emailing, phone, or other means?

Examples: High Plains (central US and Canada)

Desert

Deserts are places of arid land where precipitation is low—less than 12 inches of rainfall in a year. Although many deserts are found in the tropics, deserts, by virtue of little to no precipitation occurring there, can be found in temperate and arctic regions as well. In fact, portions of Antarctica are deserts because they have so little precipitation. In the United States there are four desert regions: the Sonoran, the Mojave, the Great Basin and the Chihuahuan. Elevation, temperature and vegetation distinguish each. Deserts cover about one fifth of the Earth's surface.

Tablelands

Related Landscape Terms: plateau, mesa, butte, fin, arch, altiplano

Tablelands are **high** flat tracts of land with steep sides. In deserts, tablelands range in declining size from plateau, mesa to butte. These are formations that have endured ages of wind and water erosion and rise up from the desert floor that literally sank around them. Their flat tops distinguish them from pointy mountain peaks and are distinctive features of desert landscapes.

As plateaus erode, other features take shape. One is the fin, a long narrow wall extending out from the plateau. This thin wall of rock further **erodes** and often a hole or window is worn into it. Should this window expand, an arch is formed.

Tablelands Questions:

1. How do you get an overview of a situation?
2. Where might you look to see through or beyond a challenge? When are your principles eroded?
3. How do you rise above difficult situations?
4. What wears you down?

Examples: Monument Valley, Utah & Arizona; Rainbow Arch, Utah (largest natural bridge in US); Grand Mesa, Colorado; Arches National Monument, Utah

Canyon

Related Landscape Terms: arroyo, chasm, gorge, gully

A deep gorge in the landscape of an arid region is known as a canyon. The gorge typically has been the result of a water flow cutting into the rock and **wearing** it down. The Grand Canyon is an example of water **working its way** down through strata of rock and creating a deep gouge in the landscape. Other names for this kind of cut into the Earth are arroyo, chasm and gorge.

Canyon Questions:

1. What do you do daily to reach your goals?
2. Evaluate your persistence and consistency.
3. What are your long- and short-term goals?
4. What has to happen for you to carve out the life you want to live?

Examples: Grand Canyon, Arizona (largest canyon in the US); Copper Canyon, Mexico; Cheddar Gorge, England

(Inland) Dune

Related Landscape Terms: hamada, erg, reg, Barchan, Seif

Because of the lack of rainfall, much of what composes tropical and temperate deserts is sand. In the Sahara, the sand rests on the erg or surface of the desert. The hamada is the desert area where the erg is exposed. If the surface is clear and has small stones and gravel instead of sand, the area is called reg.

Sand **moves** at the **whim** of wind and often forms ridges. These ridges have various shapes and names: Barchan, or crescent shaped; parabolic, or hairpin; transverse ridges; and Seif, which are long narrow ridges extending in the direction of the prevailing wind. Sand dunes move by tumbling over themselves in the wind and can appear to walk, some progressing as much as twenty feet in a year.

(Inland) Dune Questions:

1. How do you stay true to yourself?
2. In what ways do you shift to please others?
3. Describe the authentic you.
4. When do you surrender to a higher power?

Examples: Great Sand Dunes National Park, Colorado (tallest dunes in US); Death Valley; Sand Hills, Nebraska; Grand Erg Oriental, Western Sahara

Flats

Related Landscape Terms: playa, salt flat, salt lake, salt pan, chott, shatt, shott

When rain comes to the desert, there is **little to stand** in its flow as runoff. As it rolls down the sides of mesas and into arroyos, it **collects** minerals before being stopped and **held** in basins called playas on the floor of the desert. When the water **evaporates**, **salt crystals** are left in the basins and these are the salt flats.

Flats Questions:

1. Ask the flats to help you find the place of silence. Return there. This is the essence of meditation.
2. What's the difference between what you want and what you need?
3. Ask yourself, how can I change states or frame of mind?
4. Ask yourself, where do I need purification?

Examples: Bonneville Salt Flats, Utah; Black Rock Desert, Nevada

Oasis

Related Landscape Terms: well, spring

From spring or well, water means **life** and vegetation. In a desert, the oasis is the fertile place of **refreshment** and settlement and has become synonymous with water. Because of this, the oases of the desert have become the great crossroads of travelers, places of legend, caravans and exotic spices.

Oasis Questions:
1. What is your source of life?
2. How do you connect to the source of life?
3. In what ways do you thirst?
4. How do you bring life into the dry or dead places in your life?

Examples: Awjila, Libya; Kufra, Libya

Wash

Related Landscape Terms: dry wash, wadi, arroyo

This is the dried bed of a stream. Also known as a dry wash or wadi, the wash marks a place in the desert where water **once** flowed in the recent **past**.

Wash Questions:
1. What do you do to keep the past alive?
2. What, if any, is the importance of keeping the past alive?
3. How do the skeletons from your past interfere and/or contribute to your life?
4. What might you do to release the past to live more presently?

Mountains and Valleys

Mountains, the world's high places, are formed as the result of great pressure and movement within the Earth. Mountain building often takes place at the edges of the Earth's great tectonic plates, forming great systems of mountains as ranges, chains and cordilleras. Because mountains stand in the way of winds and weather, they are the great mitigators of moisture and affect climate. One side of a range can be wet much of the year while the other side can be a desert. The fact that a mountain rises up from sea level also drastically affects the flora and fauna. The higher up, the colder it gets, and vegetation can be dwarfed through exposure to the harshness, as with the krummholz—the small, prostrate trees at the upper edge of the timberline.

Folded Mountain

Related Landscape Terms: fold, overfold

As the name implies, folded mountains are formed when two tectonic plates **collide** and the Earth **folds**. When it creases with the fold pushing upward, it is called an anticline. When the fold **pushes** down, it's a syncline. Most mountain ranges are of this type, including the Appalachians.

Folded Mountain Questions:

1. In what way do you respond to a challenge? Rise to meet it? Fall before it?
2. How would you characterize your spiritual life?
3. How committed are you to connecting with the spirits?
4. What can you learn from aspiration? From inspiration?

Examples: Himalayan, Alpine, Appalachian (oldest US mountains), Andean chains

Block Mountain

Related Landscape Terms: escarpment, scarp, cliff, bluff, fault, horst, graben

Often times, **faults** in the Earth will play a role in the formation of mountains. When a block called a horst **rises** between parallel faults, a block mountain is the result.

Block Mountain Questions:

1. How do you handle pressure from multiple directions?
2. What skills do you bring that reconcile opposing or competing forces?

3. What spiritual power have you stepped into?
4. How do you deal with success? Can you simply accept a compliment?

Examples: Vosges, France; The Black Forest, Germany

Volcano

Related Landscape Terms: shield volcano, dome volcano, cinder cone, composite volcano, crater, caldera, ash cone, fumarole, puy

When **weakness** in the Earth's crust allows for magma to push upward, a conical mountain is formed that is called a volcano. Volcanoes have peculiar features and shapes based on the ways in which lava or molten rock escapes. Regarded as active, dormant or extinct, volcanoes are formed from: recurring flows of basalt, as in shield volcanoes; from viscous lava that blocks vents and causes powerful **explosions,** as in dome volcanoes; from basaltic cinder and loose ash deposited as part of a pyroclastic explosion, as in cinder cone volcanoes; and from combinations of non-explosive lava flows and pyroclastic **eruptions** in composite volcanoes. The cone of a volcano that has a bowl shaped depression is called a crater. A collapsed crater is called a caldera. Surrounding an exploded volcano is a lava field with either *aa* or *pahoehoe* lava flows solidified into lava rock.

Volcano Questions:
1. How do you handle pressure?
2. How can you transform anger into a creative force?
3. How can you communicate displeasure without being critical?
4. What is your greatest weakness?

Examples: Mt. Rainer, Washington; Mauna Loa, Hawaii; Mt. St. Helen, Washington; Fuji-san, Japan

Valley

Related Landscape Terms: river valley, rift valley, glacial valley, gulch, gully, ravine, hollow, cove, vale, dingle, dell, dale, strath

Valleys are low pieces of ground flanked by higher spots, as in a mountain or hillside. Rivers that cut into the landscape and **carve** out a groove form most valleys. Initially, the river valley is a steep-sided and sharp feature called a V-Shaped valley for the cut carved into the land. Over time, however, erosion **softens** the edges and it broadens, forming a floodplain.

Sometimes, faults are responsible for the formation of valleys. As in the case of block mountains; a block of earth called a graben can drop between two horst blocks, forming a rift valley, the most famous of which is the Rift Valley in Africa. If a glacier's gouging has been responsible for the valley, it takes its name from the distinctive shape and is called a U-shaped valley.

In many of the smaller types of valleys, such as gorges, hollows and dells, **microclimates** often form that support different varieties of flora and fauna from the surrounding areas.

Valley Questions:

1. In what ways are you protective? Of others? Of yourself?
2. What are your needs for security? Comfort?
3. What preparations have you made for the future?
4. Is there a niche you have carved out for yourself in your family? Work? Friends? Are these niches healthy?

Examples: Olduvai Gorge, Africa; Rhine Valley, Germany; Death Valley, California (one of the hottest spots on Earth); Hell's Canyon, Idaho-Oregon; King's Canyon, Sierra Nevada, California; Cheddar Gorge, England; Danakil Depression, Africa

Rocky Terrain

Related Landscape Terms: tor, crag, outcrop, outlier, clitter slope, ridge

In the high spots there are many formations that leap out in distinction. Most of them are **harder** than their surroundings and somewhat isolated in aspect. The tor is a mass of rock on the top or near the top of a hill. A crag is a rough, steep rock or point of rock. An outcrop is the portion of a rock layer that **projects** above the Earth's surface. An outlier is a mass of rock that has been separated by erosion from a similar rock mass to which it formerly was attached. When boulders break off of tors and litter the slopes below, the rocky terrain is called a clitter slope.

Rocky Terrain Questions:

1. Where are you making breakthroughs in your life?
2. Are there old issues that keep popping up?
3. What's coming to the surface that needs attention?
4. What is hard about you?

Examples: Kes Tor, Dartmoor, England; Hay Tor, Dartmoor, England; Castle Rock, Edinburgh, Scotland; Little Rock, Arkansas

Island Mountains & Hills (Inselbergs)

Related Landscape Terms: kopje, monadnock, inselberg, knob, tepui

Elevated ground that stands alone may be known as a hill or mountain; but when isolation sharpens the distinction, specialized naming underscores the feature's lone character. In South Africa, a small isolated hill is called a kopje. A little larger version found in Germany is an inselberg, known for a rounded, rocky summit rising steeply for 1,000 feet. New Hampshire's Mt. Monadnock bears the name of another isolated hill—the monadnock. And in Suriname, Tafelberg the Table Mountain is a representative of the tepuis—flat-topped mountains with steep escarpments.

Island Mountains & Hills (Inselbergs) Questions:

1. What decisions have you made about circumstances that would lead to you being singled out? Do these decisions hold you in check or free you?

2. Are there times when you wish to be the center of attention? Noticed?

3. Under what circumstances do you least wish to be noticed?

4. How do you separate yourself from others? Do you have a personal style, or do you prefer to be one of a pack?

Examples: Mount Monadnock, New Hampshire; Suilven, Scotland; Uluru and Kata Tjuta, Australia; Sugarloaf Mountain, Maryland; Tafelberg, Suriname

Hill

Related Landscape Terms: hillock, puy (volcanic hill), pingo

Other elevated bits of terrain with altitudes **lower** than mountains are called hills. There is no clear distinction between hill and mountain, except perhaps by **regional** agreement. In the United Kingdom, there are some guidelines surrounding mountains and hills. According to the Ordnance Survey system, it's a hill unless it's above 1,000 feet tall. The Oxford dictionary puts the **height** at 2,000 feet for a mountain. In the United States, 1,000 feet from base to summit makes a mountain. Hills range from 500 to 999 feet in height. A knoll is further distinguished as a hill of less than 500 feet. In Scotland, people are known to enjoy hillwalking. They trek up the highest 'hills' called Munros, which are 3,000 feet or higher and are actually mountains.

Hill Questions:

1. What is a routine challenge?

2. What strategy do you have to deal with the usual ups and downs?

3. How do you reward yourself for achievement?
4. What do you do to savor every moment, the successes and failures?

Examples: Bunker Hill; the Seven Hills of Rome (Aventine, Capitoline, Esquiline, Palatine, Quirinal, Viminal, Caelian)

Coastline

A coastline is the liminal space between the land and the ocean. It belongs to neither completely and is part of both. Coastlines by nature **fluctuate**. The action of wind and water, sun and moon all affect the aspect and appearance of this particular zone. Waves, currents and tides as well as crustal movements shape the contour of the interface, making coastlines very **dynamic systems**.

Beach

Related Landscape Terms: shore, foreshore, backshore, intertidal zone

The land area that borders the sea is called a beach. Although the typical beach is made up of sand, beaches may be composed of pebbles, rocks, boulders or mud. Each of these materials also varies. Sand, for example, may be white—a product of **pulverization** of seashells or quartz grains. Black sand is the product of **crushed** lava or **shattered** obsidian. Wind and water acting upon sand form berms and dunes.

The beach or shore has two distinct areas. The first is the foreshore or intertidal zone. This is the area of land that is marked by the extent of low tide to high tide. The second is the backshore, the portion of land covered with water beyond high tide storm. Each area forms a distinctive niche for flora and fauna.

Beach Questions:

1. You are always changing, even if it is ever so slightly. Who have you been? Who are you becoming?

2. What parts of your life are a daily grind? What parts are routine comforts?

3. What do you do to heal?

4. Is it the beach or is it the sea? What opens for you in betwixt-and-between spaces?

Examples: Nag's Head Beach, Massachusetts; Isle of Palms, South Carolina; St. Andrews Beach, Florida

Inlet

Related Landscape Terms: gulf, bay, cove, sound, arm, firth, fjord

As a result of the ocean **filling** a depression or a fracture in the Earth's crust, it often appears as if the ocean is pushing **into** the land. When this occurs, inlets are formed. Broad inlets may be gulfs, bays, or coves, while narrower inlets are termed sounds or arms.

Inlet Questions:

1. What are the voids you seek to fill? How?

2. In what situations do you allow something new to enter into your awareness?

3. How do you open to love?

4. How would you characterize your levels of openness physically, mentally, emotionally and spiritually?

Examples: Long Island Sound, New York; Gulf of Mexico; San Francisco Bay, California; Puget Sound, Washington

Headland

Related Landscape Terms: spit, cape, promontory, ness, peninsula

When the land seems to **push** its way into the ocean, headlands form. These roughly pointed pieces of land are called spits, capes, points or promontories. The most distinct type of headland is the peninsula, a piece of land surrounded on three sides by water.

Headland Questions:
1. How do you strike out into new territory?
2. When was the last time you dipped into the unknown?
3. What do you do to stay grounded or connected?
4. What, if anything, do you worry about being cut off from?

Examples: Cape Cod, Massachusetts; Land's End, England

Grotto

Related Landscape Terms: sea cave, blowhole, sea cliff

In contrast to the gentle slope of a beach, land often meets the ocean as a cliff. This steep, vertical rock face takes the full **brunt** of the ocean's activity and hollows form after years of **relentless** tides. These **hollows** eventually form caves or grottos and are subjected to water and air pressure. If there is a hole in the roof of the cave, the pressure will force water out of what is known as a blowhole.

Grotto Questions:
1. What causes you to break down physically, mentally, emotionally, or spiritually?
2. What talent or gift is burning to surface?
3. How do you protect your dreams?
4. What is your strategy for handling repetitive abuse of any nature?

Example: Blue Grotto near Capri, Italy; Molokai, Hawaii (highest sea cliffs in US)

Platform

Related Landscape Terms: arch, stack, skellig, stump, skerry

The erosive power of wave action can **separate** blocks of rock from headlands and cliffs. These lone blocks are called platforms. When these formations are subjected to erosion, hollows can form at water level, ultimately passing through the entire thickness of the platform leaving an arch behind. Arches, subject to further wave action can collapse leaving behind the two support pillars that are called stacks.

Platform Questions:

1. Under what circumstances do you lose integrity?
2. How do you protect yourself from losing energy?
3. Is there an area of your life where collapse is imminent?
4. How do you cut yourself off from the mainstream of life? Why?

Examples: Flower Pot Island, Lake Huron, Canada; The Needles, Isle of Wight, England; Haystack Rock, Oregon

Strait & Isthmus

Related Landscape Terms: strait, channel, passage, firth, tombolo

These are the **connectors**. A strait is a narrow stretch of water connecting two larger bodies of water. Its mirror is the isthmus, a narrow stretch of land connecting two larger areas of land. Also connecting land to land is the tombolo, which is a spit or bar that links an island to the mainland.

Strait & Isthmus Questions:

1. In what ways are you a connector for family and friends?
2. Characterize the way you work with the flow of energy (ideas, emotions) between people, with 'easing' on one end of the scale and 'inhibiting' on the other.

3. What is your approach to the ambiguous?

4. What are the novel ways you connect thoughts and ideas?

Examples: English Channel; Strait of Gibraltar; Isthmus of Panama; Isthmus of Suez; Llandudno, Wales (tombolo)

Open Sea

The oceans cover approximately 71% of the Earth's surface. The average depth is 5,000 meters. The ocean is divided into bodies—the Atlantic, the Pacific, the Indian and the Arctic Oceans. Certainly the water is dynamic—currents, waves, flora and fauna. But similarly **dynamic** is the sea floor that is constantly reacting to the internal pressures of the Earth through volcanic activity and plate tectonics. Subduction returns crustal material to the mantle of the Earth at the edges of continents, while new crust is spewed up from mid-ocean ridges.

The water of the ocean is affected by prevailing winds that form surface **currents** called gyres. Deeper movement of water is caused by changes in water density and temperature called thermohaline **circulation**—a process where heavier, colder, saltier water sinks and lighter, warmer, less salty water rises.

The ocean is home to plankton, microscopic life consisting of plants and animals that provide food for the larger forms of sea life. In addition to forming the **base** of the food chain, phytoplankton, the photosynthesizing microorganisms, and algae are responsible for releasing 90% of the oxygen into the atmosphere.

Island

Related Landscape Terms: eyot, island arc, key, cay, skellig, skerry

An island is an area of land **surrounded** entirely by water. Islands can be formed in several ways: an uplift of the sea floor that pushes land above the water; a drop in water level that exposes land; flooding that isolates portions of once contiguous land; erosion of portions of coastline that **isolate** portions of land; coral polyps that build up; a volcanic cone that pushes up out of the ocean. Skellig (or skeilic) is a Gaelic word used to describe a rock island out in the ocean; skerry is derived from Norse for the same. An eyot, or ait, is a small island found in the middle of a river.

Island Questions:

1. What's your idea of paradise?
2. What are some of the healthy boundaries that you maintain?
3. What do you surround yourself with for security? Friends? Busyness? Work?
4. What part of yourself do you keep only for yourself?

Examples: Hawaiian Islands, US; Cayman Islands; Easter Island

Reef

Related Landscape Terms: atoll, fringe, barrier, lagoon

When coral polyps build up over time, they rise from the ocean floor to create a reef or ridge of limestone rock. This rock, upon breaking the surface of the ocean, can become a coral island. The coral reef usually presents in one of three principle styles: a fringing reef, which grows near the shore; a **barrier** reef, which develops like a ribbon farther offshore; an atoll or ring-shaped reef, which **encloses** a lagoon. When these reefs capture shell and sand, there can be quite a build up above sea level. And, should the sea floor under a coral island undergo uplift, the island may achieve a substantial altitude.

Reef Questions:

1. How do you shelter others?
2. What do you protect in yourself?
3. What is the root of your self-protection—fear, guilt, shame?

4. In what do you place your physical, mental, emotional and spiritual safety? Evaluate the appropriateness of doing so.

Example: John C. Pennekamp Coral Reef State Park, Florida (part of the longest barrier reef in the US); Great Barrier Reef, Australia (world's largest coral reef system)

Sea Floor

Related Landscape Terms: benthic zone, trench, continental slope, continental shelf, guyot, seamount, vent

The **basin** that holds the water of an ocean is the sea floor or benthic zone. The land that gently slopes away from the land of continents and is usually shallow is called the continental shelf. At the edge of the shelf, the steep drop off descending to the ocean bed or bottom is called the continental slope. At the level of the ocean bed, there are other features. As in the desert, canyons or gorges form on the sea floor, cutting into the surface. Where volcanoes are active, trenches—or long narrow troughs—can be found, dropping below the abyssal plain or flat expanse of the ocean floor. Also, **undersea** volcanic activity results in guyots, flat-topped undersea volcanoes; seamounts, conical undersea volcanoes; and vents, areas where hot water is released.

Sea Floor Questions:

1. Describe your internal landscape, choosing from the following words: overwhelming, apprehensive, familiar, lonely, intriguing, sad, cheerful, relaxed, intimidating, depressing, frightening, gloomy, interesting, boring, angry, happy, joyful, or alert. (Use your own term if you have one that is more accurate.)

2. What are the customary contents of your internal chatter? What does this ongoing dialogue reinforce?

3. How do you attend to your needs for deep rest and deep awareness?

4. What do you consider to be the vessel that holds you in this world?

Example: Marianas Trench (the deepest part of the Ocean)

Tidal Pool

Related Landscape Terms: tide pool, rock pool

Ocean water can become trapped along a coastline when the tide recedes. These small bodies of **trapped** water are called tide pools. The balance of life in these formations is particularly **precarious**, as they are subject to excessive heat during hot summer days, a steady loss of oxygen due to little or no wave action and **fluctuating** salt levels due to evaporation or rainfall. Many species have adapted in order to live along this precarious edge. Some of the better known species that can be found in tidal pools are hermit crabs, tubeworms, sea slugs, brittlestars, sea anemones, chitons and periwinkles.

Tidal Pool Questions:

1. What part or parts of you do you consider fragile?

2. In what areas of your life do you feel things are precariously balanced? What, if anything can you do to bring security to these areas?

3. What areas of your life do you compartmentalize? Why? Are you avoiding something?

4. Under what circumstances do you feel cut off, trapped or imprisoned?

Examples: many near the rocky West Coast of the United States, especially Washington State

Shallow Water

Related Landscape Terms: pelagic zone, neritic zone, oceanic zone, epipelagic zone, mesopelagic zone

The open waters of the ocean are known as the pelagic zone. This zone is further divided into two categories—the neritic, that is the open ocean over the continental shelf; and the oceanic, that is the open ocean over the continental slope and ocean floor.

Shallower waters of these **zones** are distinguished by **depth**. The neritic zone is rich in life with the majority of fish populations living within this 125-mile thick **band** extending out from the coast to the open sea. The uppermost zone of the combined neritic and oceanic is called the epipelagic zone, and it extends downward from the surface of the ocean to about 100 meters. This is the area in which zooplankton and phytoplankton are concentrated. From 100 meters to 1,000 meters is the mesopelagic zone, the home of the giant squid (60 feet long!). Light is diminished considerably here, and it is commonly called the twilight zone. Fish, invertebrates and sea mammals are frequent visitors to this zone and often **range between** the epipelagic and mesopelagic while feeding.

Shallow Water Questions:

1. What level of ambient activity suits you? How do you cope when it is more or less?
2. What is the dance you do with your shadow side?
3. What attention do you give to your attitudes and the way that they affect others?
4. How do you allow the attitudes of others to affect you?

Deep Water

Related Landscape Terms: bathypelagic zone, abyssopelagic zone, hadal zone, deep sea trench

Ocean waters at great depth are associated with this zone. Below 1,000 meters, the waters of the ocean are frigid and devoid of light. The bathypelagic zone is from 1,000 to 4,000 meters in depth, while the abyssopelagic zone is from 4,000 meters in depth to the ocean floor. Dropping below the ocean floor is the hadal zone, the area of deep sea **trenches**. These deep waters are home to highly adapted and **otherworldly** fish and invertebrates. Around hydrothermal vents, autotrophic organisms and hyperthermophiles eke out an existence in the superheated waters, using the materials there to produce their own food and form the base of the food chain.

Deep Water Questions:

1. What is the secret you keep, even from yourself?
2. What is your strongest strategy for adapting to hardship?
3. What part of you is untouched by the world?
4. How do you approach things you don't understand?

Wild Earth

The Earth is an amazing place, sculpted and molded through the forces of wind, water and fire. The ever moving, ever changing face of the planet has a remarkable variety of the strange and miraculous, both above and below ground. The following features were selected for their exotic and evocative qualities.

Spire

Related Landscape Terms: pinnacle, hoodoo, goblin

Spires are like the steeples of great cathedrals. They are the needles that **rise up** from the desert floor and **point** to the sky.

Like sea stacks, they are rocky piles that, through erosive action, have separated from buttes and mesas, appearing to stand on their own. Many times these spires taper to a point at the top. These are pinnacles. When the tapering is irregular and the top appears thick and blocky, these pinnacles are called hoodoos or goblins.

Spire Questions:
1. What is it about you that 'sticks out like a sore thumb'? Does this work in your favor as you connect with others? Do you rely on this characteristic in some way? Does it limit you?
2. What ghosts continue to govern your thoughts, actions and choices?
3. What are you reaching for spiritually?
4. What is your belief about reaching your pinnacle of success?

Examples: Goblin Valley State Park in Utah, Bryce Canyon National Park in Utah

Karst

Related Landscape Terms: cave, sinkhole, limestone tower, cavern

Water often works its way **underground**. Streams disappear into the Earth or drop down sinkholes, sometimes called cenotes. Through mechanical abrasion and the work of mildly acidic water, limestone is carved and a distinctive landscape emerges.

The **above ground** features of this region include limestone towers and hills, poljes (large flat-bottomed depressions), dolines (hollows formed by erosion and collapse), uvalas (compound dolines) and resurgent streams all which mark the surface.

Flowing water cuts vertical shafts down into the Earth. Underground rivers flow into pools and lakes. Huge hollows are carved out, forming galleries and chambers. Dissolved minerals are **deposited** and stalactites grow from cave ceilings, stalagmites grow from the ground and the two often meet forming columns.

Karst Questions:

1. When and why do you go underground?
2. What layers have you had to build up to create beauty in your life?
3. How does your inner life express outwardly? Should it?
4. What is your relationship to time, impatience and perseverance?

Examples: Mammoth Cave, Kentucky (longest cave system in the US); The Stone Forest, Yunnan Province, China; southern Mexico (deepest most extensive cave system); Movile Cave, Romania

Badlands

Heavy rain mixed with drought can carve up land in an arid region. When this happens, rocks are sculpted into mazes of valleys that separate rocky hills that bear little or no vegetation. Erosion can be devastating. The spectacularly colored strata are characterized by steep slopes, loose soil and clay making passage through the region difficult, if not **impossible**.

Badlands Questions:

1. What do you consider impossible?
2. What is your relationship to the impossible?
3. When did you experience what you considered to be a miracle?
4. How do you confront the possibility of failure?

Example: western parts of the Dakotas and northwestern Nebraska, Badlands National Park in South Dakota

Monolith

A single **mass** of rock is called a monolith. Erosion is responsible for these **huge** stone masses which **stand out** upon a landscape.

Monolith Questions:

1. Under what circumstances do you feel overpowered or subsumed?
2. In what area of your life do you demonstrate the greatest resistance or righteousness?
3. How can you use determination to rise above a situation?
4. What's the biggest issue or challenge that you see? Are you meeting it or avoiding it?

Examples: Mount Augustus, Australia; La Pena de Bernal, Mexico; Stone Mountain, Georgia; Devil's Tower, Wyoming

Lava Flows & Other Hot Spots

Related Landscape Terms: aa, pahoehoe, lava fountain, lava plateau, pillow lava, geyser, hot spring, fumarole, lava tubes, lava cave

Volcanic activity brings molten rock to the surface to flow out and across the land. This molten rock, called magma, solidifies more quickly on the land than inside the Earth. Once hardened, two distinct types become recognizable: *aa*, which has solidified into **rough**, jagged blocks, and *pahoehoe*, which has solidified into smoother rope and cord shapes. When lava drains away from hardened surfaces, lava tubes or lava caves can form.

The heat and pressure of volcanic activity is also responsible for geysers and hot springs. Reacting to heat and pressure, water **bursts** to the surface in a geyser. If the pressure is less, the water more gently surfaces in a hot spring. If only gases are released due to heat and pressure, it is released as a fumarole.

Lava Flows & Other Hot Spots Questions:

1. How or what do you create from sudden, catastrophic change?
2. What can you do in the face of an outburst?

3. What do you do when your familiar physical, emotional, mental or spiritual territory disappears?

4. How do you initiate plans for building upon new ground?

Examples: Yellowstone National Park; Hawaii Volcanoes National Park; Craters of the Moon, Idaho; Steamboat Geyser, Yellowstone National Park (tallest geyser in US)

Salt Seas

Related Landscape Term: Seven Seas

The word sea most frequently is applied to a large expanse of salt water. Often, a small part of the ocean is called a sea. Also, an inland body of salt water is called a **salt** sea. Although the expression **'Seven Seas'** is the **ancient mariner's** expression referring to all the oceans of the world, specifically the North and South Atlantic, the North and South Pacific, the Indian, the Arctic, and the Southern oceans, it has been used by others to indicate other seas. Depending on who is counting, the seven are selected from the following nine: Adriatic Sea, Aegean Sea, Arabian Sea, Black Sea, Caspian Sea, Indian Ocean, Mediterranean Sea, Persian Gulf and Red Sea.

Salt Seas Questions:

1. How do you explore the world?

2. What mysteries are calling to you?

3. What desires have to crystallize for you to move forward?

4. What business needs to be cleaned up before you can move in a new direction?

Examples: Caspian Sea; Dead Sea

Impact Craters

Related Terms: meteor, meteorite

Occasionally, the Earth is **struck** by incoming debris. If this material **burns up** before impacting the surface of the Earth it is known as a meteor. Most meteors end up as dust that has little impact on the Earth. However, there have been incidents when large pieces of material have made it through the atmosphere and left a mark upon the land. These objects that strike the Earth are called meteorites. Although Barringer Crater is visible, many of these impact craters lie beneath the surface and have only been discovered during test drilling or other geological survey work.

Impact Craters Questions:

1. What do you think has happened when you are hit with something from out of the blue?
2. How do you cope with surprises?
3. What can you do to maintain passion for a project and avoid burn out?
4. How do you work to discover old wounds and hidden information?

Examples: Barringer Crater, Arizona; Decaturville Crater, Missouri; Chesapeake Bay Crater, Virginia; Calvin Crater, Michigan

The next Orient & Navigate suggests some simple drawing work that can help you become more intimately acquainted with each of the *terra signs*. This is not so much about grand artistry, but rather about taking time to discover your own 'seeds' for the signs.

Some Thoughts as you begin…

We have been using the name *terra sign* to talk about the individual landscapes or features. In creating your sketches, perhaps you will begin to embody the signs, sense them, and feel them in a novel way. As a reminder, a 'sign' is "an expression of meaning or sense placed within a pattern of significance." In the field of semiotics there is that which is to be signified and that which we use to signify—the signifier. In plain language, think of a platform on legs where we eat our supper (the signified), and then consider the word we use to describe this object: 'table' (the signifier). The word 'table' becomes a *sign* for us when we engage it fully and bring into our awareness all the feelings or other associations connected with it. If it is the table at our grandmother's home, it is not just a platform on legs where we eat our supper, but the place of Thanksgiving dinners, perhaps our first time at the adult table, the meal after grandpa's funeral, our first taste of grief, the vessel of family solidarity and much more. 'Table' has gathered to it the significance of a sign.

There are multiple ways in which we resonate with 'signs,' particularly those that we have called *terra signs*. This resonance draws on more than what we gather through our five senses. It incorporates feelings. So while the seed words I have highlighted in bold can guide you, and definitions are a beginning, ultimately you will abandon them for the opportunity to expand your awareness beyond the signifier into a gnosis of a different kind—perhaps make a move from head-centered knowing to heart-centered knowing. As Peter Wilberg says in his monograph *Fundamental Science and Semiotics*, "there is no dictionary we can turn to to interpret… meaning as it addresses us. For to turn to the dictionary is to sterilise…what addresses us."[6]

Orient & Navigate: The Terra Signs

Exercise #1: Finding Your Seeds

As you read the descriptions of the *terra signs* in the text, decide for yourself what is critical for you in the definition provided. This will be the basis for your 'seeds'—the words that inspire thought and introspection *for you*. Make notes in the text, highlight words in the definitions or add a new definition, and begin to answer some of the suggested questions. Take time to relate to each of the signs in your own way in order to discover personal meaning and significance.

Exercise #2: Picture It

Use the frames provided to create your special images of the *terra signs*. You may wish to begin with a given section—Freshwater, for example—or you may randomly pick what calls to you. Think about each *terra sign* and what it means to you—a rainy day hike on the bog at summer camp; a long, hot car ride to the lake for a picnic; a horrible trek up a mountain with broken shoelaces. The *terra sign* you choose to draw may be one you copy from a favorite photo or one you make up. Expand your drawings beyond the frame if you so choose, and jot down your seed words. This is a project you can revisit over time, so take your time. You may begin drawing only those *terra signs* that you know personally before moving onto others you have not experienced. Work at your own pace, in your own way. And, use whatever medium works for you—crayons, pencils, paints or markers.

Once you have explored all of the *terra signs*, you may wish to use them in cartomancy. Transfer your drawings to blank tarot cards and make a deck. Experiment with questions and lay outs. Or use your drawings as portals to the *terra signs* and enter them to seek out Makers, Keepers and Guardians.

See the following examples.

Orient & Navigate: The Terra Signs

Terra Sign: <u>Temperate Deciduous Forest</u>
Seeds:

Terra Sign: <u>Valley</u>
Seeds:

Orient & Navigate: The Terra Signs

Terra Sign: <u>Karst</u>
Seeds:

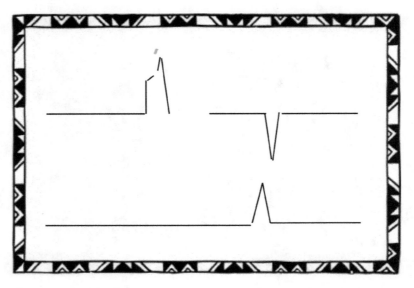

Computer line drawings can call stalactites and stalagmites to mind.

Even the signifier—desert—printed boldly calls meaning to mind.

Your Frames...use horizontally or vertically

Terra Sign:
My Seeds:

Terra Sign:
My Seeds:

9 Those Who Dwell in the Land

> *The gentle folk are not earthly people; they are a people with a nature of their own. Even in the water there are men and women of the same character. Others have caves in the rock, and in them rooms and apartments. These races were terribly plentiful a hundred years ago, and they'll come back again. My father lived two miles from here, where there were plenty of the gentle folk...Nobody could ever tell their nature exactly.*
> —Neil Colton, a Lough Derg seer, from *The Faery Faith in Celtic Countries*, by W. Y. Evans-Wentz[1]

Work with the individual *terra signs* presents an opportunity to expand your awareness of landscapes and your metaphorical way of relating to them. But this is still merely scratching the surface. Journey work will take you into deeper understanding of the beings that are associated with and inhabit the landforms. One way to come into closer rapport with those with whom we cohabitate is to shift our focus even more deeply into the land.

Eliade makes a distinction between the yogi and the shaman that supports this shift into the land. In *Shamanism: Archaic Techniques of Ecstasy*, he describes the difference between a yogi and a shaman in the following way. The yogi's practice has the goal of enstasis, that is, a final concentration of the spirit in order to escape from the cosmos: this is a flight from the Earth, our Mother, who births us and nurtures us. The shaman on the other hand, seeks ecstasy, what we call the journey, which takes him through various cosmic regions, including the Earth.[2] This underscores the prejudice of many Westerners when engaged in spiritual practices; we have been trained to look up and away from the Earth. This was touched upon lightly in Chapter 1 in the discussion of the desacralization of the Earth by the Abrahamic religions. It is reinforced by our attachment to the tale of Heaven—the place up above, milk and honey, Paradise, the afterlife, the pie in the sky when you die. It is, however, not limited to the three pervasive traditions of *the* Book. It has also infiltrated much of what can be called New Age philosophy, which is based in part on Asian Indian yogic practice. There is a focus up and away from the Earth, a calling down of light from above, an 'upcentric' and 'outcentric' approach to finding inspiration and connection to the Creator or All That Is. Certainly, we are affected by what is up and out. However, closer to home, are those beings and partners that are down and in. It's about balance.

In looking for guidance as we pursue this downward and inward path, it's not the tale of Hell or Inner Earth we are tracking, but rather what lives in Faery Seership. Building on the cosmic regions or zones outlined in Chapter 6, the World Tree not only connects the Lower, Middle and Upper Worlds; it connects the light or sun found in each of these worlds—the Middle World sun as Sol, but also as the fire in each individual heart. As our thinking shifts to this way of understanding, light not only comes from within us and is showered down from above, but flows upward from the land as well. It is through diving into and working within this Earthlight that we will encounter our cohabitants. As Orion Foxwood has said, there is a star that burns beneath our feet.[3]

One may wonder about the validity of these explorations and where to find the maps that guide the quest. As Westerners, we are poorly trained, or so we think, when it comes to traveling such realms. We may feel impoverished or jealous of people like the Huichol, who have rituals that teach their children the signposts they will use as adults when they travel into the realms with peyote. Joan Halifax in *Shamanic Voices* writes about "Plays the Drum and

Flies the Children to the Land of Peyote," the chanted ceremony that teaches children the cosmic geography of the journey to the Sacred Land of Peyote. The children at the close of the ceremony have a mental map of the territory they have traversed, and one that plots their path for future journeys.[4] But where, we ask, are our maps?

Our maps do exist, though we may have to open our eyes to see them. They exist in the forms of fairy tales and myths, many of which we have heard since childhood, where the hero or heroine experiences basic human challenges and needs to conquer obstacles to progress and reach his or her goal. Much has been written of Arthurian legend and the quest for the Grail, for example, centerpieces for our Western maps into realms beyond the surface world. Beyond these tales are the oral traditions of song and ballad, which are our guides on our inner journeys to our goals if we but learn to see them in a different way. In fact, any rousing tale where the good guy wins in a righteous and moral way can become a map. Think of George Lucas's *Star Wars* or Tolkien's *Lord of the Rings*. It is learning to see the tale at a deeper level that provides the clues to what Joseph Campbell calls the "hero's journey."

An example of this kind of deeper or tiered interpretation and mapping is evident in the navigation practices of the Polynesians. James Barr writes of his experiences in "Of Metaphysics and Polynesian Navigation," an article that inspired John Perkins's book *Psychonavigation*. As a cook working on cargo vessels in Polynesia, Barr noticed that his captain used no sextant and did little that Barr recognized, as a sailor himself, to determine his craft's direction or position. In seeking further information, and after learning Samoan, he came to learn that the finer art of reading the sea and navigating was based on three different levels he termed literal, moral and anagogical. The literal level involves the intimacies of the obvious: clouds, flight of sea birds, color of the sea, the taste of the water. Understanding the subtle aspects of these phenomena took years of practice. The moral level engaged the deity behind the phenomena—Tuaraati, the Ocean Lord. His help was invoked to guide the mind of the navigator. The third level, the anagogical, is the point at which the navigator merged with the sea in every possible way and became the sea. For the navigators, this merging was accomplished through the breath, producing an altered state of consciousness Barr compares to zazen, a kind of Buddhist meditation. It is in this state that the navigator communed directly with the Lord of the Waves and came to know his location.[5]

To learn from our tales and myths we must follow the same process. We begin by understanding the plot details and characters—a very literal approach. We go deeper when we begin to apprehend the controlling principles that guide and direct, and see them as symbolic of elements acting in our lives. When we merge with the story and allow it meaning in our own life and use it to inform us as we pursue our life path, we are working with the anagogical. It is at this level that the transformation occurs, appearing as magic, and our lives are changed.

As we work with stories, common elements emerge representing the altered state. Often, the inward or downward realms are represented as going down a tunnel, crossing water or alighting upon an island. This corresponds with the shamanic technique of entering a tunnel to reach the Lower World.

Aside from the awareness of up and down, a common thread woven through the geography of the worlds is the four directions. It is universal for a human to look left, right, before and behind to locate him or herself in space. Each of these directions, when oriented to an Earthly magnetic pole or the movement of the Sun, becomes North, East, South and West. These directions become more than a compass guiding one along the surface of the Earth. Each direction also encodes deeper meaning and has other ordinary and non-ordinary reality associations. We have encountered these associations in Chapter 6's Orient & Navigate. As a reminder, for one Native American tradition the spirit paths of the directions are:

North, for healing the physical being through cleansing, renewal and purification; East, for healing the mental being through illumination, clarity and wisdom; South, for healing emotions through examination of growth, trust and love; and West, for healing the spiritual level of life through introspection, experience and illumination.[6] For the Celtic seer, there are four rivers, each flowing into and out from the seer's position on the Earth. For the Irish Celt, there are four cities, each associated with a direction and scope of influence. Ulster is in the North and influences battle; Leinster is to the East and influences prosperity; Munster is to the South and influences music; and, Connacht is to the West, influencing knowledge.[7] Each '4' is imbued with meaning and can be a tool to glean further insights.

The Elements and Elementals

In Chapter 5 we encountered the Makers, those elements that are the verbs of the Earth: Earth, Air, Fire and Water. On the visible level, the Makers are represented in their purest, ordinary reality forms: rock, wind, flame and wave. Yet, each has a non-ordinary reality identity that can be perceived in the shamanic state of consciousness. Each of these stands with other related beings, all working below the surface—behind the scenes—to bring the slice of reality we perceive on a daily basis into view so that our physical aspect can experience and our spiritual aspect can grow. Physical reality is not only the land upon which we walk, but also our physical body. All the elements are active so that we have structure and can breathe, digest and cry. But we are also exposed to the elements on our journeys, where we learn that we are more than the body we inhabit. According to Kyriacos Markides in his contact with Daskolos, a wise teacher on Cyprus, one may be exposed to the elements on a journey—exomatosis as Daskolos calls it—to learn that one is not bound by them.[8] In his tradition, the novices undergo several initiations for each of the four elements to learn various lessons, such as tolerance and patience (from Earth) and living outside the material body through vivid dreams (from Water).

Teachings that predate political or state Christianity in Europe, as well as tales and legends from that time, are rife with beings that exist in ordinary and non-ordinary reality who are associated with the elements and directions. Names of these creatures color the language of stories: sylphs (air), leviathans (water), the Phoenix (fire) and trolls (earth), to name a few. Each elemental creature plays a role in the duality of the Maker it expresses. Just as air can cleanse and inspire, it can also destroy or overwhelm. Water may purify within an unchanging course, or it may stagnate or drown. The passion of fire can express in righteousness and justice or, conversely, in rage, hate and despair. And Earth can create and lovingly nurture, or lead to rot and sterility. The two paths—one leading to the light and one leading away—are essential to the land and its forms but may require that we work to balance or mitigate the effects of interacting with the beings expressing light or darkness.

However, before one can leap in to balance or harmonize the Earth—rather an inflated view of our place and power as humans—it is important to look beyond the human-centric point of view and get to know the non-human neighbors one might encounter. The presumption that 'we should [interfere] because we can' is an arrogant approach to the Earth and the intelligent beings that live in (ordinary and non-ordinary reality Middle World) and under (non-ordinary reality Lower World) the land. The table found in the Appendix lists some of the beings known from myth and legend who have strong associations with certain landforms or *terra signs*. It is very possible that these cohabitants may be encountered when journeying into the land and landscapes. In reading the list, which barely scratches the surface, it can be noted that there are numerous beings who have been named and about whom tales have been written, all with origins in the ethnic heritages of many Westerners. Some have even found their way into popular culture through books and films like *Harry Potter* and *Lord of the Rings*. We carry this knowledge deep within and may find many of these creatures familiar—friendly or fearsome. Not all of these creatures are about light and love, yet neither are all humans. These beings, like humans, follow their individual or collective paths toward or away from light according to their natures. Our task is to know them as they are and learn to make alliances when and where appropriate. This is done respectfully over many interactions with the guidance of our helping spirits.

Once you've reviewed the table, you'll likely notice that in many cases, distinctions are difficult to make between beings. Names overlap and associations to landscapes are shared. The point of the table is not to provide an absolute directory of the beings one may encounter in spirit work with landscapes, but rather to highlight the associations of particular beings with the landscapes that they inhabit or guard. Also noteworthy is that many of these beings are presented from a European point of view. Another list with African, Asian and indigenous American cohabitants would double the list at the very least. While helpful in demonstrating elemental associations with landscapes, the associations in the table are not meant to overshadow the fact that there are indigenous traditions from around the world with their own expressions of our Earthly cohabitants. The Little People of the Cherokee are but one example.

What these beings represent is a complex set of relationships between the physical and the spiritual, between themselves and the Makers, and ultimately between themselves and the Creator. For the European forebears who historically lived close to the land, its intelligence and consciousness appeared to them as the beings listed in the Appendix. What we know from our work with journeys is that often an identity that is shared with us from non-ordinary reality isn't an absolute identity, but rather one that we can usefully comprehend according to our own development and the resonance of our heart. What if each of the beings listed was perceived through the eyes of someone who arrived here on Earth with a fuller understanding of energy exchange, knew and appreciated the balance between creation and destruction, and chose to harmonize with all beings? Perhaps this visitor to Earth would 'see' these elemental beings in a different way. They might be less human in appearance and of a different order than our minds currently can embrace.

Earlier, I alluded to the idea of balancing and mitigating the effects of interacting with beings expressing light or darkness. Many times we humans try to 'fix' things according to our point of view without regard for 'who' or 'what' is present before we jump to intervene. To enter the realms of our non-ordinary cohabitants and presume that we know what is best is to be an unschooled guest who perhaps does not deserve the gift of hospitality. We have to learn who and what are in a place and respect what's there before we can begin to have influence and make wise contributions. As the Australian Aborigines might say, the land has its own dream and perhaps our task is to help uncover that dream rather than impose ours.

In the final Orient & Navigate we will explore that dream and those who work to implement it.

Orient & Navigate: Those Who Dwell in the Land

Exercise #1: Who You Know

Even if we didn't always *believe,* we all grew up with a smattering of contact with the idea of cohabitants. Think about the scary stories you were told as a child, what you did when you lost a tooth, how you celebrated Yule. List some of the cohabitants you encountered either in reality or via book or imagination.

Exercise #2: Favorite Tales

Make a list of your favorite tales that include beings with whom we share the Earth. What makes them your favorite tales? Are there tales you really *don't* like that include cohabitants? What about these tales colors your feelings?

Exercise #3: Cohabitants

To begin to develop intimacy with the land, the Earth and Its dream, try the following.

Journey to a place on the Earth. Seek the beings living there and ask them what they do to preserve the harmony and balance of that specific Ordinary Reality place.

After taking this journey a number of times, you may wish to ask how you can support the beings you have met in their tasks to maintain harmony and balance.

Date:

Place:

Notes:

Orient & Navigate: Those Who Dwell in the Land

✂ **Exercise #4: Homes Under Threat**

Recall the tale from the Dolomites that talked of interaction with the Salwans, the dwarves displaced by invaders (Chapter 3). Can you imagine what it would be like to be displaced from your special place, your homeland? Think of a local spot that may have been *someone's* home or is *someone's* home currently under threat. Visit it in ordinary reality or on a journey and see if you can find traces of the cohabitants involved. Perhaps you can contact them and ask if there is some way you can support them. (Caution: This is not about 'fixing' a situation by offering your space or some other space as a homeland. There are beings in *those* places that would need to be consulted. This is about acting in ordinary reality to protect certain spots. The real question is: How willing are you to stand up to protect places that need ordinary reality help?)

✂ **Exercise #5: The Directions—Establishing Sacred Space**

Sit in a quiet place in nature. Using a compass, locate each of the cardinal directions. Begin by facing the East and asking it to help you understand the gifts it brings to you. Avoid thinking about specific systems of meaning for this. The idea of specific qualities of the directions has been discussed in Chapter 6. In this exercise, you are looking for a very personal influence that East wraps around you, how East seeps into your skin. Take notes. Is there a being associated with the East? Is there a Maker associated with the East?

Proceed to the South, West and North asking to understand the gifts and influence each of the directions contributes to your life.

Orient & Navigate: Those Who Dwell in the Land

You may wish to do this over the course of four days so that you can give adequate attention to each.

Upon completion you may wish to move on to include Up and Down.

Now, with these gifts in mind, write a prayer acknowledging (in honor and gratitude) each of the directions. This prayer can be used to establish ceremonial space—some would call it 'calling the quarters'—or as a way to honor the incredible power and help that surrounds you as well as to enlist its support. You may use this as a way to begin a ceremony.

Date:
Place in Nature:

East:

South:

West:

North:

Up:

Down:

Prayer:

Afterword: Only the Tip of the Iceberg…

Landscapes explored via the journey and used in divination are part of a rich stream of information that broadens the view we have of our universe—both its ordinary and non-ordinary aspects. We are gifted with knowledge through our efforts, and hopefully that knowledge is forged into wisdom that we take into our daily lives. With increased awareness we can begin to notice the many aspects of Mother Earth—the *terra signs*—and use them to find greater significance and meaning. This is the heterogeny of Mircea Eliade as recalled from Chapter 2; appreciating the variations has the potential of opening our hearts to the sacred.

There are many trails to follow when we enter into the study of landscapes. We have only scraped the surface in our explorations here. Yet to be pursued is the path deep into the heartland of our forebears and descendents, where we can access ancestral or familial perceptions in order to bring healing to our lineages. Another path takes us to the thin places like Iona, Scotland, where the veil between the worlds is said to be thin and contact with other worlds and the divine is but a breath away. The path of the pilgrim also awaits, wending its way through sacred landscapes touching upon the numinous, replicating cosmography, while the land itself tests and initiates the seeker.

Study of the sciences of geomancy and *feng shui*, too, can contribute to our understanding of place and space. They are tools used to read and adjust energy flows that can affect one's fortune and health. Lithopuncture likewise strives to reestablish harmony.

The scope of this book, however, has been limited to presenting ways to connect to the Earth, to rebuild familiarity and intimacy with Her and all those who inhabit Her, multidimensionally. In working with Her many faces—the *terra signs*—it is hoped that you have discovered new ways to approach your home and the beings living there with an open and compassionate heart.

Some time ago, I was thinking of 'space' and 'place' and all the special spots on Mother Earth I had been blessed to visit. My thoughts burst out in the following way.

With or Without Walls

I can enter either way, through the flame, a nighttime campfire perhaps,
crackling with impatience for me to open the doorway
and step wide-eyed into the non-time of vision.
Or the water can call to me,
seducing me with her potent murmur to merge,
dive deep down into her cool silent embrace
and fall into an alert sleep of closed eyes
where dreams play with memories on a private screen.

Either way I enter the most sacred of spaces—
a place not bound but bountiful—filled with all that was and ever will be:
a place of light and dark, pushing one against the other, with me always.

Memory collides with recall
begging to know, was it now or then?
Neither terribly important in the end,
merely an exercise for the organs of perception
calling to mind all those spots on my Mother's body
where my small touch was felt and recorded many times.
Ah, Avebury. Again.
Tall stones compelling the rise of a palpable tension.
Was it because I was a blind boy
bidden to perform a weighty role in a long forgotten religion?

Or, was it because I was a young woman
facing the might of a decision to change my life
and walk my talk in a new way?
I can feel the power of the stones,
especially the one with the bright green and purple lines of energy
rippling vertically across the surface,
charging at once into the sky and into the ground.
I can see that stone eyes open or closed;
the memory cuts like the knife borne in the hand of the blind boy
obliged to enter the circle through the letting of blood.

Boots beat out a rhythm on the hard, packed earth
a soldier in the Emperor's army,
marching in the cold gusts of Britannia's many gales.
It's the Wall this time. Expected to keep out Picts.
Ten feet wide at the base, milecastles and watchtowers,
strung like pearls on a silken thread, drape across the landscape.
It looks fragile, but has weathered storms of all kinds,
lasting well beyond the dispute.
Like most warriors, the beer and camaraderie fortify my spirits.
We drank and ravaged our way across the countryside, mates to the end.
So strange that in this flash of today, the same is true.
I face walls erected in ages long forgotten to keep certain demons at bay
yet, find them to be illusions forged of a fear that was never my own.
I fight to dismantle them.
I caress pearls. A gift given in the shadow of the Wall.
In the reverse of yesterday, the Wall is an opening to new horizons.

The damn sand gets everywhere; my eyes, ears and throat ache.
Dry as it is, I love the rich colors at twilight which soothe like a fine plum wine.
I am intoxicated.
From the back of this smelly, ungrateful and unholy ship of the desert
I survey the endless Sahara dunes.

In my lightheaded giddiness I grip my camel's saddle tightly.
The sky is so deep and the land so vast,
I could be pulled into the vacuum of relative
infinity if I'm not careful.
A nighttime meal beckons.
Soon I have the vestiges of civilization around me,
defining me as the human I think I am.
With walls, I feel brave. Without walls, alive.

Another desert? That must be Crestone. High desert this time.
Looking into the night sky, I was really alive, alert to tingling.
The exotic of this venue well beyond spices and language and dress.
I search the sky for something not of the Earth,
hoping to contact that outside myself so far as to bring me to myself.
Lights. I'm alive. Sounds. I'm alive.
Closed-eye patterns of electrical interference. I am alive.
Among the stars. I am alive.

It comes fast and furious now.
In a story, I am alive.
In a creek, I am alive.
In a musty, canvas tent, I am alive.
In the tall trees shadowed by Mount Washington, I am alive.
All places are sacred for me.
I am there.
I am alive!

Slowly and peacefully, I recall who I am at this time.
I blink my eyes against sparks from the fire.
I resurface with a rush of inhaled breath.
I depart my Self to re-enter myself and sigh—
gratitude for the breadth of my experience.
Blessed.
I am alive.

—spr

Appendix—
Table of Cohabitants[1]

Elemental Being	Elemental Association	Other Names
Alseid	Earth	Greece; nymphs of glens and groves
Alven	Water	Netherlands; also, Ottermaaner; water faeries of ponds, lakes and rivers
Auloniad	Earth	Greece; nymph of mountain pastures and vales
Ballybogs	Earth	Ireland, England, Wales; guardians of bogs; also sometimes caves; small mud-covered creatures with spindly arms
Banshee	Water	Ireland, Scotland, Germany; also, Bean Sidhe, Washer of the Shrouds, Washer at the Ford; found near dark rivers, trees & stones; appear as young maiden, matron, or hag
Boggart	Earth	also, Hobgoblins, Bogans, Bauchans, Gobelins, Bogey Man, Boogies, Padfoot, Hobbers, Bobs, Blobs; Scotland; squat male dwarf; associated with fields and marshes
Brownies	Earth	Britain, Denmark, Russia, Canada, US; also, House Brownie, Bogle, Hobs, Little Man, Nis, Domovoi, Dobie, Killmoulis, Bookha, Bwca, Finland; Tomtra, Tighe, Fenoderee; appear as wrinkled, brown, shaggy man
Camenae	Water	Roman; goddesses of springs, wells, fountains
Crinaeae	Water	Greece; naiads of fountains
Drac	Water	France, Germany, England; damp mossy caves; appear as floating purple blob, chalice or female humanoid
Dragon	Fire	Greece, Europe, China; also, Balaur, Basilisk, Y Ddraig Goch, Guivre, Lindworm, Vere Celen, Vouivre, Wurm, Wyvern, Zmey, Zmiy, Zmaj, Zmeu; large winged serpent or reptile, with or without legs; Slavic versions have multiple heads
Drake	Fire	Western fire dragon; smell like rotten eggs and chicken coops
Dryad	Earth	Greece; female tree spirits, specifically the oak tree
Dwarf	Earth	Icelandic; reported in The Eddas; smiths to the gods; also, Dvergr; live in the mountains and earth
Eleionomae	Water	Naiads of marshes

Elemental Being	Elemental Association	Other Names
Elf	Earth	Scotland, Ireland, Wales, Scandinavia, Europe; also, Elb, Erl, Mannikin, Fair Folk, Good Neighbors, Green Children, Old People, Silent People; faery people of forests, caves; appear humanoid and human-sized with pointed ears
Ellyllons	Water	Wales; small inland lakes; faeries
Erdmanleins	Earth	German; goblin
Field Faeries	Earth	
Fir Darrigs	Water	Ireland, Scotland; also, Rat Boys, Fear Dearg; swamps, raths (fairy mounds), marshes; fat, ugly faeries with dark hairy skin, snouts and tails; carry a shillelagh topped with a skull
Fire Faeries	Fire	
Flower Faeries	Earth	
Fossegrim	Water	Norway; waterfalls and fjords; small humanoids with feet tapering off into nothing
Ghillie Dhu	Fire	Scotland; also, Gillee Doo or Yoo; guardian tree spirits disguised as foliage
Giant	Earth	Greece, Germany; guardians of hills, mountains, rivers and forests
Gnome	Earth	Germanic; the primary Earth-type elemental; Ghob is king of the gnomes; many varieties of gnomes; 15 cm humanoid with tall pointy caps
Goblins	Earth	Europe: also, Gobblin, Gobeline, Gobling, Goblyn, Gobbelin, Gobelin, Hobgobs, Hob-thrush, Blobins, Bogies, Bogles, Brags, Boggarts, Trows, Spriggans, Knockers, Kobolds, Wichtlein, Phooka; Greece; often associated with grottoes; humanoid, 30 cm tall and hairy
Grindylow	Water	English; also, Grundylow; connected to meres, bogs and lakes; also pits, ponds and wells; long sinewy arms
Gryphon	Earth/Air	also, griffin; Middle East; part mammal, part bird; power in Earth and Sky
Gwyllion	Earth	Wales; mountain faeries; small and man-like; also, Gwyllon
Hamadryad	Earth	Greece; also, Hamadryadniks; nymph bonded until death to a specific tree

179

Elemental Being	Elemental Association	Other Names
Heather Pixies	Earth	Scotland, England; also, Moor Pixies; moors and heather; appear with golden auras and translucent wings
Huldrafolk	Earth	Scandinavia; damp caves in the mountains; have dark brown tongues; also, Skogsfru, Skovfrue, Tusser; also, forest dweller
Iele	Fire	Romanian; lived in sky, forest, caves, isolated mountain cliffs, marshes
Jinn		also, jinni, djinni, djinn, genie; pre-Islamic Arabia; beings of smokeless fire
Kelpies	Water	Ireland, Germany, Scotland; also, Nicker, Uisge; often took the form of horses; north seas, rivers and lochs; shape-shifters; appear as 1/2 horse & 1/2 fish, horse, monster or human; also, Bäckahästen, Each-uisge, Cabbyl-ushtey, Nykur
Knocker	Earth	Wales, Cornwall, South Central Europe; also, Coblynau, Wichlein, Para, Black Dwarves, Koblenigh, Tommyknocker; goblin; inhabit caves and mines; knock and make silly faces
Kobold	Earth	Northern European; goblin; also, Kobolde, Kobauld, Cobauld, Coblynau, Hütchen, Heinzelmännchen, Nis, Niägruisar, Para; inhabit hollow trees, caves & mines; dwarf faeries
Korrigan	Earth	Brittany, Cornwall; also, Corrigans, Korils, Poulpikans, Teuz, Korrikaned; cliffs, especially near the shore of Brittany; appear as little ugly men with 2 horns, goat hooves and cat claws
Leimakid	Earth	Greek; a type of nymph of the meadows
Leprechaun	Earth	Ireland; also, The Gentry, Fir Darrig, Clurichaun, Cluricaune, Logherima; springs and grassy hills; solitary dwarf male; Italy, Monaciello
Lesidhe	Air	Ireland; also, Leshes; Russia, Zuibotshniks, Leshiye; Vodyaniye; guardians of forests; appear as an owl, wolf or disguised as foliage
Leviathan	Water	also, sea serpent; large creature similar to a crocodile with teeth and fire-breathing
Limnades	Water	Greece; naiads of lakes
Mary Player	Water	Greece, Germany, England; also, Merewipers, Meerweibers, Lorelei; lives near cliffs; lovely young female faery
Meliai	Earth	Greece; also, Meliae; female tree spirits, specifically the ash tree

Elemental Being	Elemental Association	Other Names
Merpeople	Water	also, Mermaids, Mermen, Water Dancers, Fish Folk, Blue Men, Merrows, Murduchu; vast caves especially Atlantis; 1/2 fish & 1/2 human
Moss People	Earth	Germany, Switzerland; also, Greenies; woodlands; appear with butterfly wings on small human body
Naiad	Water	Greece; a type of nymph presiding over fountains, wells, springs, streams, brooks (flowing water)
Napaeae	Earth	Greece; nymphs of wooded valley, glens or grottoes
Nereid	Water	sea (salt water) nymphs; the 50 daughters of Nereus and Doris; ex. Aktaie, the nereid of the sea-shore, Amphitrite, the nereid of the sea-caves; blue-haired, beautiful maidens
Nisse	Earth	Scandinavian
Nixen	Water	Germany, Switzerland; also, Urchins, Nis; river and water sprites
Nixies	Water	German & Scandinavian sprites of lakes and streams; fresh water nymphs; usually in human form
Noggles	Water	Italy; streams and rivers; appear as small grey horse
Nuckelavee	Water	Scotland; also, Nuchlavis; Scotland; seashore
Nymphs	Multiple	Greece; celestial nymphs, water nymphs, land nymphs, plant nymphs, underworld nymphs; associated with mountains, groves, springs, rivers, trees, valleys, grottoes
Oceanids	Water	Greece; the 3000 children of Oceanus and Tethys; each a patron of a particular spring, river, ocean, lake, pond, pasture, flower or cloud
Ogres	Earth	also, Orculli, Norrgens; a kind of giant; larger than humans with excessive hair and humped backs
Oread	Water	Greece; nymphs living in mountains, valleys, or ravines
Pegaeae	Water	Greece; naiads of springs

Elemental Being	Elemental Association	Other Names
Phooka	Earth	Ireland, Cornwall, Channel Islands; a type of goblin with large human head and pig, horse or goat body; shape-shifter, usually showing dark fur; also, Púca, Pooka, Phouka, Phooca, Púka, Pwca, Pwwka
Pillywiggins	Air	Isle of Man, Wales; flower faeries and spring faeries; seen as small winged creatures
Pixie	Air	Scotland, Cornwall; also, Urchins, Pisgies, Piskies, Pigseys, Pechts, Pechs, Pickers, Grigs, Dusters; a trooping Fay; flower gardens; appear as small winged creatures; also, Pixy, Pixi; sometimes associated with high moorland and underground at ancient ancestor sites
Portune	Earth	England; also, Wish Makers; woodlands; appear as old men, the smallest of faeries
Potameides	Water	Greece: naiads of rivers
Rubezahl	Air	Germany, Eastern Europe; also, Hey-Hey Men, Hoioimann, He-Manner, Huaman, Schlocherl, Rubezahl; German and Eastern mountains; male dwarfs in black coats with walking sticks
Salamander	Fire	also, Saleerandees; Medieval tradition; the primary Fire-type elemental; Djinn is king of the salamanders; scaled faeries like bipedal lizards
Selkies	Water	Shetland Islands & Iceland; also, Roanes; spirits taking the form of gray seals that can shed skin to become beautiful young women or men; ocean and lochs
Shellycoats	Water	Scotland; pools of fresh water, especially woodland lakes; look fish-like
Spriggan	Earth	Cornwall; goblin; small humanoids guarding hill treasure
Sprite	Air	Europe; also, Spriggan; broad term used for faeries, such as elves or dwarves
Storm Faeries	Air	
Sylph	Air	the primary Air-type elemental; Paralda is the king of the sylphs
Thussers	Earth	Norway; earthen mounds near fjords; small humanoid faeries
Tomte	Earth	Scandinavia; Nisse, Tomtenisse, Tonttu; three foot tall, long white beard, colorful clothes
Tree Elves	Earth	

Elemental Being	Elemental Association	Other Names
Troll	Earth	Sweden, Denmark; also, Trold, Trow, Hill Men, Berg People, Rise, Jutul, Tusse; generic term for Scandinavian elf; tall, thin, great age & skill; live in caves and hills and guard bridges and by-ways; huge and hard skinned
Trow	Earth	Scotland; goblin; squat, misshapen faeries with no legs
Undine	Water	Greece; the primary Water-type elemental; Niksa, Nicksa or Nixsa is the king of the undines
Water Faeries	Water	
Water sprites	Water	
Wight	Earth	Norse mythology; also, Sea-wight, Landwight, Landvættir, Huldufólk, Tomte, Nisse; appear as small humanoids
Wood Elves	Earth	also, Gianes; Italy; found in woodlands; humanoid wearing peasant clothing
Wyvern	Fire	also, Dragon; winged serpent with two or no legs
Yallery Brown		England; nature spirit, ragged man with yellow-brown skin

Endnotes

Introduction

1. Mircea Eliade, *The Sacred and the Profane*, Trans. Willard R. Trask, Harcourt Brace Jovanovich, New York & London, 1959, p. 140.

2. Eliade, *The Sacred and the Profane*, p. 141.

3. Waldemar Bogoras, "The Chuckchee-Religion," *Memoirs of the American Museum of Natural History,* Volume XI, Leiden, E. J. Brill Ltd., New York, 1904, p. 281.

4. Lee Carroll, *Kryon: Partnering with God,* The Kryon Writings, Inc., Del Mar, 1997, p. 296. The phrase 'sweet spot' has been used in the Kryon materials to signify the idea of spiritual contract and deployment. That is, if one is following one's contract with Spirit, one is said to be in one's 'sweet spot.' My use of the term is more directly tied to one's relationship with specific places which may or may not be part of a spiritual contract or deployment.

5. Eric Weiner, *The Geography of Bliss,* Twelve, New York & Boston, 2008, pp. 35-37.

Chapter One: All Our Relations

1. John Grim and Mary Evelyn Tucker, "Series Forward," *Indigenous Traditions and Ecology,* Ed. John A. Grim, Harvard University Press, Boston, 2001, p. 4.

2. Julio Valladolid and Frédérique Apffel-Marglin, "Andean Cosmovision and the Nurturing of Biodiversity," *Indigenous Traditions and Ecology,* Ed. John A. Grim, Harvard University Press, Boston, 2001, p. 656.

3. Ed McGaa, Eagle Man, *Native Wisdom,* Four Directions Publishing, Minneapolis, 1995, p. 232.

4. Mircea Eliade, *The Sacred and the Profane*, p. 139.

5. Carl Sagan, *Pale Blue Dot: A Vision of the Human Future in Space,* Random House, New York, 1994, pp. 3-9.

6. Eliade, *The Sacred and the Profane*, pp. 141-144.

7. Kwasi Konadu, "Adinto: Akan Naming and Outdooring Ceremony," 2010, https://sites.google.com/site/afropedia/adinto-akan-naming-and-outdooring-ceremony (Last accessed 11/21/13.)

8. Eliade, *The Sacred and the Profane*, p. 140.

9. Ogbu U. Kalu, "The Sacred Egg: Worldview, Ecology, and Development in West Africa," *Indigenous Traditions and Ecology*, Ed. John A. Grim, Harvard University Press, Boston, 2001, p. 233.

10. Javier Galicia Silva, "Religion, Ritual, and Agriculture among the Present-Day Nahua of Mesoamerica," *Indigenous Traditions and Ecology*, Ed. John A. Grim, Harvard University Press, Boston, 2001, p. 319.

11. Mircea Eliade, *Rites and Symbols of Initiation: The Mysteries of Birth and Rebirth*, Trans. Willard R. Trask, Spring Publications, Dallas, 1958, p. 31.

12. Eliade, *The Sacred and the Profane*, pp. 143–144.

13. According to Ed McGaa, an Oglala Sioux writer and teacher of Native American spiritual ways, there are seven ceremonies that serve as a foundation for various prayers to the Creator. These are: the Pipe Ceremony, the Sweat Lodge, the Vision Quest, the Sun Dance, the Making of Relatives, the Giveaway and the Yuwipi Spirit Calling. Each has a specific purpose and an underlying organizing structure to support the prayers of the people. See McGaa, *Native Wisdom*, pp. 107–131.

14. Mircea Eliade, *Shamanism: Archaic Techniques of Ecstasy*, Trans. Willard R. Trask, Princeton University Press, Princeton, 1964, pp. 45–46.

15. Eliade, *Shamanism*, p. 58.

16. Jack Farrell, *Mystical Experiences: Wisdom in Unexpected Places from Prisons to Main Street*, Park East Press, New York, 2011, p. 147.

17. Orion Foxwood, *The Tree of Enchantment: Ancient Wisdom and Magic Practices of the Faery Tradition*, Weiser Books, San Francisco & Providence, 2008, pp. 97–99. Lord Orion includes specific instructions for creating a Soul Pot to hold the soil from ancestral graves.

18. Natasha Beskhlebnaya, "Sleeping on Graveyards," *Russian Life*, May/June 2007, pp. 53–58 (Last accessed via www.russianlife.com 3/27/14.)

19. Beskhlebnaya, p. 58.

20. Manduhai Buyandelger, *Tragic Spirits: Shamanism, memory, and gender in contemporary Mongolia*, University of Chicago Press, Chicago, 2013, pp. 62–63.

21. Paul Devereux, *Shamanism and the Mystery Lines,* Llewellyn Publications, St. Paul, 1993, p. 115.
22. Walter L. Brenneman, Jr., "Holy Wells of Ireland," *The Power of Place,* Ed. James A. Swan, Quest Books, Wheaton, 1991, p. 138.
23. Brenneman, p. 139.
24. David Cloutier, Ed. *Spirit Spirit: Shaman Songs,* Copper Beech Press, Providence, 1980, pp. 39–40. The poem written by Cloutier is titled *Song about the Spirit of the Sea.* It is a wonderful rendition of a song recorded by Waldemar Bogoras in his Memoirs of the American Museum of Natural History. The subject is the "Spirit Woman who lives beneath the waves" and feeds everyone with her bounty. It is a song of honor and respect for the goddess Sedna without whom, the people could not eat.
25. Edward and Wendy Esko, *Macrobiotic Cooking for Everyone,* Japan Publications, Tokyo, 1980, pp. 64–66.
26. Eliot Cowan, *Plant Spirit Medicine,* Swan·Raven & Company, Newberg, 1995, p. 64.
27. Daniel Stokols, "People-Environment Relations: Instrumental and Spiritual Views," *The Power of Place,* Ed. James A. Swan, Quest Books, Wheaton, 1991, pp. 351–352.
28. John A. Grim and Mary Evelyn Tucker, "Series Forward," *Indigenous Traditions and Ecology,* Ed. John A. Grim, Harvard University Press, Boston, 2001, p. xxv.
29. Eliade, *The Sacred and the Profane,* pp. 151–152.
30. Grim and Tucker, p. xxv.
31. Dell DeChant, *The Sacred Santa: Religious Dimensions of Consumer Culture,* Wipf & Stock, Eugene, 2002, pp. 53–68.
32. DeChant, pp. 88–100.
33. James Mooney, *The Ghost Dance Religion and Wounded Knee,* Dover Publications, Inc., Mineola, 1973, p. 721.
34. Eliade, *The Sacred and the Profane,* p. 65.

Chapter Two: The Shaman & Divination
1. Dennis Danvers, *The Watch,* HarperCollins Publishers, New York, 2002, p. 67.
2. Richard Feather Anderson, "Geomancy," *The Power of Place,* Ed. James A. Swan, Quest Books, Wheaton, 1991, p. 194.
3. Anderson, p. 195.

4. Mircea Eliade, *The Sacred & The Profane*, p. 37.

5. Danvers, p. 109.

6. Stanislav Grof, *SHAMANISM: Archaic Techniques of Healing and Ecstasy,* unpublished paper, Section II.

7. Avvakum Petrovich, "The Shaman: A 'Villain of a Magician Who Calls Demons,'" *Shamans Through Time: 500 Years on the Path to Knowledge,* Eds. Jeremy Narby and Francis Huxley, Jeremy P. Tarcher/Putnam, New York, 2001, p. 18.

8. Jeremy Narby, "Shamans and Scientists," *Shamans Through Time: 500 Years on the Path to Knowledge,* Eds. Jeremy Narby and Francis Huxley, Jeremy P. Tarcher/Putnam, New York, 2001, pp. 301–305.

9. Carlos Castañeda, *The Teachings of Don Juan: A Yaqui Way of Knowledge,* Pocket Books, New York, 1995, p. 209–210.

10. Mircea Eliade, *Shamanism,* p. 417.

11. Mircea Eliade, *Shamanism,* pp. 173, 259.

12. See Andrew Neher, "A Physiological Explanation of Unusual Behavior in Ceremonies Involving Drums," *Human Biology,* Vol. 34, May 1962; Barbara W. Lex, "The Neurobiology of Ritual Trance," *The Spectrum of Ritual: A Biogenetic Structural Analysis,* Eugene G. d'Aquili, Charles D. Laughlin, Jr., John McManus, Columbia University Press, New York, 1979.

13. Felicitas Goodman, *Where The Spirits Ride the Wind,* Indiana University Press, Bloomington & Indianapolis, 1990, pp. 14, 86.

14. Michael Harner, *The Way of the Shaman,* Harper and Row, San Francisco, 1990, p. xix.

15. Harvey Alden, *Dreamkeepers: A Spirit-Journey into Aboriginal Australia,* HarperCollins, New York, 1994, p. 3–4.

16. Frank G. Speck, *Naskapi: The Savage Hunters of the Labrador Peninsula,* University of Oklahoma Press, Norman, 1977, p. 194–196.

17. Julian Jaynes, *The Origin of Consciousness in the Breakdown of the Bicameral Mind,* Houghton Mifflin Company, Boston, 1976, pp. 236–245. While his major thesis has been discredited, the distinctions he draws regarding the forms of divination are still useful.

18. H. Spencer Lewis, *Self-Mastery and Fate with the Cycles of Life,* Grand Lodge of the English Language Jurisdiction, AMORC, Incorporated, 1982. The entire book is filled with data for evaluating the fortune of given hours, days, years, etc.

19. Stephen T. Chang, *The Tao of Balanced Diet: The secrets of a Thin & Healthy Body,* Tao Publishing, San Francisco, 1987, pp. 41–43.

20. Jaynes, p. 239.

21. Philip L. Ravenhill, *The Self and the Other: Personhood and Images among the Baule, Côte d'Ivoire,* Fowler Museum of Cultural History, Monograph Series Number 28, University of California, Los Angeles, 1994, p. 24.

22. The Three Initiates, *The Kybalion: A Study of Hermetic Philosophy of Ancient Egypt and Greece,* The Yogi Publication Society, Chicago, 1940, p. 113.

23. The Three Initiates, p. 119.

24. The Three Initiates, p. 122.

25. Michio Kaku, *Physics of the Impossible: A Scientific Exploration into the World of Phasers, Force Fields, Teleportation, and Time Travel,* Anchor Books, New York, 2009, p. 60.

26. Isaac Bonewitz, *Real Magic,* Samuel Weiser, Inc., York Beach, 1989, p. 6.

27. Bonewitz, p. 6.

28. Speck, pp. 142–163.

29. Speck, pp. 168–169.

Chapter Three: Myth, Morality & Ethics

1. Ralph Waldo Emerson, "Nature," *Essays,* Grosset & Dunlap, New York, (undated edition), p. 159.

2. Joseph Campbell, *Transformations of Myth Through Time,* audio program, Vol. 1, Program 2, 1989.

3. Gregory Cajete, "Indigenous Education and Ecology: Perspectives of an American Indian Educator," *Indigenous Traditions and Ecology,* Ed. John A. Grim, Harvard University Press, Boston, 2001, p. 636.

4. Walter L. Brenneman, Jr., "Holy Wells in Ireland," *The Power of Place,* Ed. James A. Swan, Quest Books, Wheaton, 1991, p. 137.

5. http://www.enwikipedia.org/wiki/BookofLeinter (Last accessed 10/3/13.)

6. Caitlín and John Matthews, *The Encyclopedia of Celtic Wisdom: A Celtic Shaman's Sourcebook,* Element Books, Rockport, 1994, pp. 7–16.

7. http://www.summerlans.com/crossroads/library/dindsenc.htm (Last accessed 10/3/13.)

8. Sarah Lyall, "Building in Iceland? Better Clear it with the Elves First," http://www.newyorktimes.com/2005/07/13/international/europe/13elves.html?ei=5070&en=e183bced40b78d72 (Last accessed 7/14/205.)

9. Richard Craze, *Feng Shui Game Pack*, Godsfield Press, New Alresford, 1999, p. 14.

10. James A. Swan, "Befriending the Dragon," *The Power of Place*, Ed. James A. Swan, Quest Books, Wheaton, 1991, pp. 207, 209.

11. Swan, p. 210.

12. Kazuo Matsubayashi, "Spirit of Place: The Modern Relevance of an Ancient Concept," *The Power of Place*, Ed. James A. Swan, Quest Books, Wheaton, 1991, p. 335.

13. Matsubayashi, p. 336.

14. Peter Jordan, "The materiality of shamanism as a 'world-view': Praxis, artefacts and landscape," *Archaeology of Shamanism*, Ed. Neil Price, Routeledge, London & New York, 2001, p 89.

15. Jordan, p. 90.

16. Jordan, p. 95.

17. J. Peter Brosius, "Local Knowledges, Global Claims: On the Significance of Indigenous Ecologies in Sarawak, East Malaysia," *Indigenous Traditions and Ecology*, Ed. John A. Grim, Harvard University Press, Boston, 2001, p. 128.

18. Brosius, p. 129.

19. Brosius, pp. 134–135.

20. Brosius, p. 135.

21. Brosius, p. 136.

22. Brosius, p. 138.

23. Brosius, p. 150.

24. Brosius, pp. 150–152.

25. Keith Basso, "Wisdom Sits in Places: Notes on Western Apache Landscape," *Senses of Place*, Eds. Steven Feld and Keith Basso, School of American Research Press, Santa Fe, 1996, p. 73.

26. Basso, pp. 68–69.

27. Basso, p. 61.

28. Basso, p. 60.

29. Basso, pp. 62–63.

30. Basso, pp. 64–65.
31. Bruce Chatwin, *The Songlines*, Penguin Books, New York, 1987, p. 269.
32. Matsubayashi, pp. 339–340.
33. Chatwin, p. 269.
34. Chatwin, pp. 45, 57, 73.
35. Chatwin, p. 60.
36. Chatwin, pp. 77–78.
37. Chatwin, pp. 106–107.
38. Karl Felix Wolff, *The Dolomites and Their Legends*, Verlagsanstalt Athesia, Bozen, 1958, pp. 7–49.

Chapter Four: The Metaphoric & the Metachoric

1. Felicitas D. Goodman, p. 79.
2. Faith Popcorn, http://www.faithpopcorn.com/, Trendbank (Last accessed 10/17/13.)
3. Mircea Eliade, *Shamanism*, pp. 173, 259.
4. Paul Devereux, *Shamanism and the Mystery Lines: Ley Lines, Spirit Paths, Shape-Shifting & Out-of-body Travel*, Llewellyn, St. Paul, 1993, pp. 160–161.
5. Devereux, pp. 160–163.
6. Devereux, p. 210.
7. Devereux, p. 212.
8. G. William Domhoff, http://www2.ucsc.edu/dreams/Library/senoi5.html (Last accessed 10/17/13.) Domhoff in his discussion of the debunked Senoi Dream Theory investigates the work of LaBerge. His comment is that LaBerge was the most successful one participating in his (LaBerge's) studies and few other studies have attempted to demonstrate dream control.
9. Michael Talbot, *The Holographic Universe*, Harper Perennial, New York, 1991, pp. 48–50.
10. Richard Katz, *Boiling Energy*, Harvard University Press, Cambridge & London, 1982, pp. 41–42.
11. Katz, pp. 94–95.
12. Katz, pp. 102, 106.

13. Martha Ward, "What in the world is conjure?" (personal correspondence), *Voodoo Queen: The Spirited Lives of Marie Laveau*, University Press of Mississippi, Jackson, 2004.

14. James Mooney, pp. 783, 798–799.

15. http://www.boxingscene.com/motivation/3507.php (Last accessed 10/17/13.)

16. Belinda Gore, *Ecstatic Body Postures: An Alternate Reality Workbook*, Bear & Company, Rochester, 1995, p. ix.

17. For some lessons and experiences with mandalas see Rudiger Dahlke's *Mandalas of the World: A Meditating & Painting Guide*, Sterling Publishing Co., Inc., New York, 1992.

18. Nevill Drury, *Exploring the Labyrinth: Making Sense of the New Spirituality*, Continuum, New York, 1999, pp. 107–108.

19. Talbot, p. 70.

Chapter Five: What is a Landscape?

1. Orion Foxwood, *The Faery Teachings*, Muse Press, 2003, p. 87.

2. As we delve into a discussion of landscape, it may be useful to look at space and place. While the words are somewhat interchangeable, a phenomenological geographical school of thought would distinguish them. Space is the medium that holds action. Space may divided into forms such as somatic space (how the upright human body experiences senses and movement); perceptual space (how an individual links intentionality to bodily movement and involves feelings, memories, awe, emotion, wonder); existential space (lived space, the concrete experiences of individuals socialized within a group, determining Otherness); architectural space (deliberately created and bound space); and, cognitive space (the ground for reflection). Place takes on a more personal meaning as it is the ground of human experiences, feeling and thought; personal and cultural identity are tied to place. "Most significant places are located or positioned in space." See Christopher Tilley, "Space, Place, Landscape and Perception: Phenomenological Perspectives," *A Phenomenology of Landscape*, Berg Publishers, Oxford & Providence, 1994, pp. 8–17.

3. William Becker and Bethe Hagens, "The Planetary Grid: A New Synthesis," *Pursuit*, Vol. 17, No. 2, Second Quarter, 1984, pp. 50–54. See also, http://en.wikipedia.org/wiki/Timaeus(dialogue)#Golden_ratio (Last accessed 1/6/14.) In this Platonic dialogue, the philosopher Timaeus discusses the elements as building blocks of nature and assigns related solids to each: tetrahedron for fire, octahedron for air,

icosahedron for water and cube for earth. The dodecahedron is given as the shape God used for the universe.

4. 4. http://en.wikipedia.org/wiki/Golden_ratio (Last accessed 1/6/14.) The Greeks viewed beauty as an ideal—the perfection represented by symmetry, proportion and harmony, very 'godly' qualities.
5. 5. http://en.wikipedia.org/Vitruvian_man (Last accessed 1/6/14.)
6. 6. http://en.wikipedia.org/Fibonacci_numbers#In_nature (Last accessed 1/6/14.)
7. 7. Carlos Castañeda, p. 94.
8. 8. Mark A. Trahant, "Creating Sacred Places," *American Indian*, Smithsonian Institution, Spring 2005, p. 34.
9. 9. Marko Pogačnik, *Sacred Geography: Geomancy: Co-creating the Earth Cosmos*, Lindisfarne Books, Great Barrington, 2007, p. 35.
10. 10. Pogačnik, pp. 221–228.

Chapter Six: The Work of the Shaman: Journeying & Divination

1. Mircea Eliade, *The Sacred and the Profane*, p. 36.
2. Michael Harner, *Cave and Cosmos*, North Atlantic Books, Berkeley, 2013, p. 48.
3. Harner, *Cave and Cosmos*, p. 48.
4. John Matthews, *The Winter Solstice*, Quest Books, Wheaton, 1998, p. 181.
5. Foxwood, *The Faery Teachings*, p. 133.
6. Verrier Elwin, *The Religion of an Indian Tribe*, Oxford University Press, Oxford, 1955, p. 68.
7. For additional help with the journey see: Michael Harner, *Cave and Cosmos*, pp. 241–247; Tom Cowan, *Shamanism as a Spiritual Practice for Daily Life*, The Crossing Press, Freedom, 1996, pp. 40–50.
8. For more help with the Middle World Journey see Cowan, pp. 86–88.
9. See Harner, *Cave and Cosmos*, pp. 224–231; Cowan, p. 56.
10. Jordan, p. 92.
11. Elwin, p. 244.
12. Michael D. Fischer, "Anthropological Studies of Divination: Spider Divination," http://lowie.kent.ac.uk/Divination/Spider/index.html (Last accessed 1/6/14.)

13. JD, "Lessons Learned from Tony Robbins," *Sources of Insight,* http://sourcesofinsight.com/lessons-learned-from-tony-robbins/ (Last accessed 10/18/13.)
14. Elizabeth Moran and Val Biktashev, *The Complete Idiot's Guide to Feng Shui,* Alpha Books, New York, 1999, p. 214.
15. Sun Bear, Wabun Wind & Crysalis Mulligan, *Dancing with the Wheel: The Medicine Wheel Workbook,* Simon & Schuster, New York, 1991, pp. 4–5, ff.
16. Jamie Sams, *The Sacred Path Workbook,* HarperSanFrancisco, New York, 1991, pp. 36–39.
17. Sun Bear, et al, pp. 49–50.
18. Kenneth Meadows, *Earth Medicine,* Element, Boston, 1996, p. 43.
19. Sams, pp. 40–43.
20. Meadows, p. 50.
21. Sun Bear, et al, pp. 51–52.
22. Sams, pp. 44–47.
23. Meadows, p. 53.
24. Sun Bear, et al, pp. 52–53.
25. Meadows, p. 57.
26. Sams, pp. 48–51.
27. Sun Bear, et al, pp. 48–49.

Chapter Seven: Into the Picture

1. Christopher Tilley, p. 74.
2. Eric Hirsch, "Landscape: Between Place and Space," *The Anthropology of Landscape,* Eds. Eric Hirsch and Michael O'Hanlon, Clarendon Press, Oxford, 1995, p. 2.
3. Nicholas Green, "Looking at the Landscape: Class Formation and the Visual," *The Anthropology of Landscape,* Eds. Eric Hirsch and Michael O'Hanlon, Clarendon Press, Oxford, 1995, p. 37.
4. *Mary Poppins,* Directed by Robert Stevenson, Produced by Walt Disney, Screenplay by Bill Walsh & Don DaGradi. Based on *Mary Poppins* by P. L. Travers, 1964.
5. *Alice in Wonderland,* Directed by Norman Z. McLeod, Produced by Emanuel Cohen, Screenplay by Joseph L. Mankiewicz and William

Cameron Menzies. Based on *Alice's Adventures in Wonderland* and *Through the Looking Glass* by Lewis Carroll, 1933.

6. Robert Monroe, *The Gateway Experience: Guidance Manual,* The Monroe Institute, Faber, 1995, p. 6.

7. http://www.symbols.com/encyclopedia/28/281.html (Last accessed 11/4/13.)

8. http://www.symbols.com/encyclopedia/27/274.html (Last accessed 11/4/13.)

9. Ted Andrews in his book *Enchantment of the Faerie Realm,* Llewellyn Publications, St. Paul, 2001, pp. 211–213, has also suggested using these symbols and small variations on such to open doorways to the Faerie Realm.

10. http://www.symbols.com/encyclopedia/14/146.html (Last accessed 11/4/13.) This is a Chinese ideogram for river or stream.

11. http://www.symbols.com/encyclopedia/22/225.html and http://www.symbols.com/encyclopedia/22/2223.html (Last accessed 11/4/13.) This is a sign for the burning fire sometimes associated with Vesta's altar.

Chapter Eight: The Terra Signs

1. Fredric Lehrman, *The Sacred Landscape,* Celestial Arts, Berkeley, 1988, p. 13.

2. Hirsch, p. 23.

3. Darrell Addison Posey, "Intellectual Property Rights and the Sacred Balance: Some Spiritual Consequences from the Commercialization of Traditional Resources," *Indigenous Traditions and Ecology*, Ed. John A. Grim, Harvard University Press, Boston, 2001, pp. 10–13.

4. The definitions in this section are an amalgam of information compiled from the following sources:

    - *Natural Wonders of the World,* Eds. Richard L. Scheffel, Susan J. Wernert, The Reader's Digest Association, Inc., Pleasantville, 1980.

    - Encarta Encyclopedia, 2002.

    - *American Nature: Our Intriguing Land and Wildlife,* Ed. Barbara J. Morgan, The Reader's Digest Association, Inc., Pleasantville, 1997.

5. William Longgood, *The Queen Must Die,* W.W. Norton & Company, Inc., London & New York, 1985, pp. 215–216.

6. Peter Wilberg, "Fundamental Science and Semiotics," 2002, http://newgnosis.co.uk/inniverse/semiotics.html (Last accessed 11/6/13.)

Chapter Nine: Those Who Dwell in the Land

1. W.Y. Evans-Wentz, *The Fairy Faith in Celtic Countries,* Citadel Press, New York, 1994, p. 73.
2. Mircea Eliade, *Shamanism,* p. 417.
3. Foxwood, *The Faery Teachings,* pp. 21, 55.
4. Joan Halifax, *Shamanic Voices,* Arkana, New York, 1979, p. 233–237.
5. James Barr, "Of Metaphysics and Polynesian Navigation," *Avaloka,* Vol. III: 1 and 2, Grand Rapids, Winter 1988/Summer 1989, pp. 3–8.
6. See the endnotes for Chapter 6, n. 7–19.
7. Frank MacEowen, *The Spiral of Memory and Belonging,* New World Library, Novato, 2004, pp. 110–111.
8. Kyriacos C. Markides, *Homage to the Sun,* Arkana, New York, 1987, p. 159.

Appendix – Cohabitants

1. This table is an amalgam of information from multiple sources including:
   - Ted Andrews, *Enchantment of the Faerie Realm;* Orion Foxwood, *The Faery Teachings;* http://www.monstropedia.org (last accessed 1/3/07).
   - Brian Froud and Alan Lee, *Faeries,* Peacock Press/Bantam Books, New York, 1979.
   - Theresa Bane, *Encyclopedia of Fairies in World Folklore and Mythology,* McFarland & Company, Publishers, Jefferson, 2013; http://selkywolf.com/sweetsong/fairydictionary.html (last accessed 2/12/14), http://www.bellaterreno.com/art/default.aspx (last accessed 2/12/14).

Bibliography

Alden, Harvey, *Dreamkeepers: A Spirit-Journey into Aboriginal Australia*, HarperCollins, New York, 1994.

Anderson, Richard Feather, "Geomancy," *The Power of Place*, Ed. James A. Swan, Quest Books, Wheaton, 1991.

Andrews, Ted, *Enchantment of the Faerie Realm*, Llewellyn Publications, St. Paul, 2001.

Bane, Theresa, *Encyclopedia of Fairies in World Folklore and Mythology*, McFarland & Company, Inc., Jefferson, 2013.

Barr, James, "Of Metaphysics and Polynesian Navigation," *Avaloka*, Vol. III: 1 and 2, Grand Rapids, Winter 1988/Summer 1989.

Basso, Keith, "Wisdom Sits in Places: Notes on Western Apache Landscape," *Senses of Place*, Eds. Steven Feld and Keith Basso, School of American Research Press, Santa Fe, 1996.

Becker, William and Bethe Hagens, "The Planetary Grid: A New Synthesis," *Pursuit*, Vol. 17, No. 2, Second Quarter, Little Silver, 1984.

Beskhlebnaya, Natasha, "Sleeping on Graveyards," *Russian Life*, May/June 2007. (Last accessed via www.russianlife.net 3/27/14.)

Bogoras, Waldemar, "The Chuckchee-Religion," *Memoirs of the American Museum of Natural History*, Volume XI, Leiden, E. J. Brill Ltd., New York, 1904.

Bonewitz, Isaac, *Real Magic*, Samuel Weiser, Inc., York Beach, 1989.

Brenneman, Walter L., Jr., "Holy Wells of Ireland," *The Power of Place*, Ed. James A. Swan, Quest Books, Wheaton, 1991.

Brosius, J. Peter, "Local Knowledges, Global Claims: On the Significance of Indigenous Ecologies in Sarawak, East Malaysia," *Indigenous Traditions and Ecology*, Ed. John A. Grim, Harvard University Press, Boston, 2001.

Buyandelger, Manduhai, *Tragic Spirits: Shamanism, memory, and gender in contemporary Mongolia*, University of Chicago Press, Chicago, 2013.

Cajete, Gregory, "Indigenous Education and Ecology: Perspectives of an American Indian Educator," *Indigenous Traditions and Ecology*, Ed. John A. Grim, Harvard University Press, Boston, 2001.

Campbell, Joseph, *Transformations of Myth Through Time*, audio program, Vol. 1, Program 2, 1989.

Castañeda, Carlos, *The Teachings of Don Juan: A Yaqui Way of Knowledge*, Pocket Books, New York, 1995.

Chang, Stephen T., *The Tao of Balanced Diet: The Secrets of a Thin & Healthy Body*, Tao Publishing, San Francisco, 1987.

Chatwin, Bruce, *The Songlines*, Penguin Books, New York, 1987.

Cloutier, David, Ed., *Spirit Spirit: Shaman Songs*, Copper Beech Press, Providence, 1980.

Cowan, Eliot, *Plant Spirit Medicine*, Swan, Raven & Company, Newberg, 1995.

Cowan, Tom, *Shamanism as a Spiritual Practice for Daily Life*, The Crossing Press, Freedom, 1996.

Craze, Richard, *Feng Shui Game Pack*, Godsfield Press, New Alresford, 1999.

Dahlke, Rudiger, *Mandalas of the World: A Meditating & Painting Guide*, Sterling Publishing Co., Inc., New York, 1992.

Danvers, Dennis, *The Watch*, HarperCollins Publishers, New York, 2002.

DeChant, Dell, *The Sacred Santa: Religious Dimensions of Consumer Culture*, Wipf & Stock, Eugene, 2002.

Devereux, Paul, *Shamanism and the Mystery Lines: Ley Lines, Spirit Paths, Shape-Shifting & Out-of-body Travel*, Llewellyn, St. Paul, 1993.

Domhoff, G. William, "Senoi Dream Theory: Myth, Scientific Method, and the Dreamwork Movement," March 2003, http://www2.ucsc.edu/dreams/Library/senoi5.html (Last accessed 10/17/13.)

Drury, Nevill, *Exploring the Labyrinth: Making Sense of the New Spirituality*, Continuum, New York, 1999.

Eliade, Mircea, *Rites and Symbols of Initiation: The Mysteries of Birth and Rebirth*, Trans. Willard R. Trask, Spring Publications, Dallas, 1958.

Eliade, Mircea, *The Sacred and the Profane*, Trans. Willard R. Trask, Harcourt Brace Jovanovich, New York & London, 1959.

Eliade, Mircea, *Shamanism: Archaic Techniques of Ecstasy*, Trans. Willard R. Trask, Princeton University Press, Princeton, 1964.

Elwin, Verrier, *The Religion of an Indian Tribe*, Oxford University Press, Oxford, 1955.

Emerson, Ralph Waldo, "Nature," *Essays*, Grosset & Dunlap, New York, (undated edition).

Esko, Edward and Wendy, *Macrobiotic Cooking for Everyone*, Japan Publications, Tokyo, 1980.

Evans-Wentz, W.Y., *The Fairy Faith in Celtic Countries*, Citadel Press, New York, 1994.

Farrell, Jack, *Mystical Experiences: Wisdom in Unexpected Places from Prisons to Main Street*, Park East Press, New York, 2011.

Fischer, Michael D., "Anthropological Studies of Divination: Spider Divination," http://lowie.kent.ac.uk/Divination/Spider/index.html (Last accessed 1/6/14.)

Foxwood, Orion, *The Faery Teachings*, Muse Press, Coral Springs, 2003.

Foxwood, Orion, *The Tree of Enchantment: Ancient Wisdom and Magic Practices of the Faery Tradition,* Weiser Books, San Francisco & Providence, 2008.

Froud, Brian and Alan Lee, *Faeries,* Peacock Press/Bantam Books, New York, 1979.

Goodman, Felicitas, *Where The Spirits Ride the Wind,* Indiana University Press, Bloomington & Indianapolis, 1990.

Gore, Belinda, *Ecstatic Body Postures: An Alternate Reality Workbook,* Bear & Company, Rochester, 1995.

Green, Nicholas, "Looking at the Landscape: Class Formation and the Visual," *The Anthropology of Landscape,* Eds. Eric Hirsch and Michael O'Hanlon, Clarendon Press, Oxford, 1995.

Grim, John and Mary Evelyn Tucker, "Series Forward," *Indigenous Traditions and Ecology,* Ed. John A. Grim, Harvard University Press, Boston, 2001.

Grof, Stanislav, *SHAMANISM: Archaic Techniques of Healing and Ecstasy,* unpublished paper, Section II.

Halifax, Joan, *Shamanic Voices,* Arkana, New York, 1979.

Harner, Michael, *Cave and Cosmos,* North Atlantic Books, Berkeley, 2013.

Harner, Michael, *The Way of the Shaman,* Harper and Row, San Francisco, 1990.

Hirsch, Eric, "Landscape: Between Place and Space," *The Anthropology of Landscape,* Eds. Eric Hirsch and Michael O'Hanlon, Clarendon Press, Oxford, 1995.

Jaynes, Julian, *The Origin of Consciousness in the Breakdown of the Bicameral Mind,* Houghton Mifflin Company, Boston, 1976.

JD, "Lessons Learned from Tony Robbins," *Sources of Insight,* http://sourcesofinsight.com/lessons-learned-from-tony-robbins/ (Last accessed 10/18/13.)

Jordan, Peter, "The materiality of shamanism as a 'world-view': Praxis, artefacts and landscape," *Archaeology of Shamanism,* Ed. Neil Price, Routledge, London & New York, 2001.

Kaku, Michio, *Physics of the Impossible: A Scientific Exploration into the World of Phasers, Force Fields, Teleportation, and Time Travel,* Anchor Books, New York, 2009.

Kalu, Ogbu U., "The Sacred Egg: Worldview, Ecology, and Development in West Africa," *Indigenous Traditions and Ecology,* Ed. John A. Grim, Harvard University Press, Boston, 2001.

Katz, Richard, *Boiling Energy,* Harvard University Press, Cambridge & London, 1982.

Konadu, Kwasi, "Adinto: Akan Naming and Outdooring Ceremony," 2010, https://sites.google.com/site/afropedia/adinto-akan-naming-and-outdooring-ceremony (Last accessed 11/21/13.)

Lehrman, Fredric, *The Sacred Landscape,* Celestial Arts, Berkeley, 1988.

Lewis, H. Spencer, *Self-Mastery and Fate with the Cycles of Life,* Grand Lodge of the English Language Jurisdiction, AMORC, Incorporated, 1982.

Lex, Barbara W., "The Neurobiology of Ritual Trance," *The Spectrum of Ritual: A Biogenetic Structural Analysis,* Eugene G. d'Aquili, Charles D. Laughlin, Jr., John McManus, Columbia University Press, New York, 1979.

Longgood, William, *The Queen Must Die,* W. W. Norton & Company, Inc., London & New York, 1985.

Lyall, Sarah, "Building in Iceland? Better Clear it with the Elves First," http://www.newyorktimes.com/2005/07/13/international/europe/13elves.html?ei=5070&en=e183bced40b78d72 (Last accessed 7/14/2005.)

MacEowen, Frank, *The Spiral of Memory and Belonging,* New World Library, Novato, 2004.

Markides, Kyriacos C., *Homage to the Sun,* Arkana, New York, 1987.

Matsubayashi, Kazuo, "Spirit of Place: The Modern Relevance of an Ancient Concept," *The Power of Place*, Ed. James A. Swan, Quest Books, Wheaton, 1991.

Matthews, Caitlín and John, *The Encyclopedia of Celtic Wisdom: A Celtic Shaman's Sourcebook*, Element Books, Rockport, 1994.

Matthews, John, *The Winter Solstice*, Quest Books, Wheaton, 1998.

McGaa, Ed, Eagle Man, *Native Wisdom*, Four Directions Publishing, Minneapolis, 1995.

Meadows, Kenneth, *Earth Medicine*, Element, Boston, 1996.

Mooney, James, *The Ghost Dance Religion and Wounded Knee*, Dover Publications, Inc., Mineola, 1973.

Monroe, Robert, *The Gateway Experience: Guidance Manual*, The Monroe Institute, Faber, 1995.

Moran, Elizabeth and Val Biktashev, *The Complete Idiot's Guide to Feng Shui*, Alpha Books, New York, 1999.

Morgan, Barbara J., Ed., *American Nature: Our Intriguing Land and Wildlife*, The Reader's Digest Association, Inc., Pleasantville, 1997.

Narby, Jeremy, "Shamans and Scientists," *Shamans Through Time: 500 Years on the Path to Knowledge*, Eds. Jeremy Narby and Francis Huxley, Jeremy P. Tarcher/Putnam, New York, 2001.

Neher, Andrew, "A Physiological Explanation of Unusual Behavior in Ceremonies Involving Drums," *Human Biology*, Vol. 34, May 1962.

Petrovich, Avvakum, "The Shaman: A 'Villain of a Magician Who Calls Demons,'" *Shamans Through Time: 500 Years on the Path to Knowledge*, Eds. Jeremy Narby and Francis Huxley, Jeremy P. Tarcher/Putnam, New York, 2001.

Pogačnik, Marko, *Sacred Geography: Geomancy: Co-creating the Earth Cosmos*, Lindisfarne Books, Great Barrington, 2007.

Popcorn, Faith, http://www.faithpopcorn.com/, Trendbank (Last accessed 10/17/13.)

Posey, Darrell Addison, "Intellectual Property Rights and the Sacred Balance: Some Spiritual Consequences from the Commercialization of Traditional Resources," *Indigenous Traditions and Ecology*, Ed. John A. Grim, Harvard University Press, Boston, 2001.

Ravenhill, Philip L., *The Self and the Other: Personhood and Images among the Baule, Côte d'Ivoire*, Fowler Museum of Cultural History, Monograph Series Number 28, University of California, Los Angeles, 1994.

Sagan, Carl, *Pale Blue Dot: A Vision of the Human Future in Space*, Random House, New York, 1994.

Sams, Jamie, *The Sacred Path Workbook*, HarperSanFrancisco, New York, 1991.

Scheffel, Richard L. and Susan J. Wernert, Eds., *Natural Wonders of the World*, The Reader's Digest Association, Inc., Pleasantville, 1980.

Silva, Javier Galicia, "Religion, Ritual, and Agriculture among the Present-Day Nahua of Mesoamerica," *Indigenous Traditions and Ecology*, Ed. John A. Grim, Harvard University Press, Boston, 2001.

Speck, Frank G., *Naskapi: The Savage Hunters of the Labrador Peninsula*, University of Oklahoma Press, Norman, 1977.

Stokols, Daniel, "People-Environment Relations: Instrumental and Spiritual Views," *The Power of Place*, Ed. James A. Swan, Quest Books, Wheaton, 1991.

Sun Bear, Wabun Wind & Crysalis Mulligan, *Dancing with the Wheel: The Medicine Wheel Workbook*, Simon & Schuster, New York, 1991.

Swan, James A., "Befriending the Dragon," *The Power of Place*, Ed. James A. Swan, Quest Books, Wheaton, 1991.

Talbot, Michael, *The Holographic Universe*, Harper Perennial, New York, 1991.

Three Initiates, The, *The Kybalion: A Study of Hermetic Philosophy of Ancient Egypt and Greece*, The Yogi Publication Society, Chicago, 1940.

Tilley, Christopher, "Space, Place, Landscape and Perception: Phenomenological Perspectives," *A Phenomenology of Landscape*, Berg Publishers, Oxford & Providence, 1994.

Trahant, Mark A., "Creating Sacred Places," *American Indian*, Smithsonian Institution, Washington, Spring 2005.

Valladolid, Julio, and Frédérique Apffel-Marglin, "Andean Cosmovision and the Nurturing of Biodiversity," *Indigenous Traditions and Ecology*, Ed. John A. Grim, Harvard University Press, Boston, 2001.

Ward, Martha, "What in the world is conjure?" (Personal correspondence.)

Ward, Martha, *Voodoo Queen: The Spirited Lives of Marie Laveau*, University Press of Mississippi, Jackson, 2004.

Weiner, Eric, *The Geography of Bliss*, Twelve, New York & Boston, 2008.

Wilberg, Peter, "Fundamental Science and Semiotics," 2002, http://newgnosis.co.uk/inniverse/semiotics.html (Last accessed 11/6/13.)

Wolff, Karl Felix, *The Dolomites and Their Legends*, Verlagsanstalt Athesia, Bozen, 1958.

Filmography

Alice in Wonderland, Directed by Norman Z. McLeod, Produced by Emanuel Cohen, Screenplay by Joseph L. Mankiewicz and William Cameron Menzies. Based on *Alice's Adventures in Wonderland* and *Through the Looking Glass* by Lewis Carroll, 1933.

Mary Poppins, Directed by Robert Stevenson, Produced by Walt Disney, Screenplay by Bill Walsh & Don DaGradi. Based on *Mary Poppins* by P. L. Travers, 1964.

Playtime, Directed by Jacques Tati, Produced by Bernard Maurice, René Silvera, Screenplay by Art Buchwald, Jacques Lagrange, Jacques Tati, 1967

Web References

http://www.bellaterreno.com/art/default.aspx (Last accessed 2/12/14.)

http://www.boxingscene.com/motivation/3507.php (Last accessed 10/17/13.)

http://www.enwikipedia.org/wiki/BookofLeinter (Last accessed 10/3/13.)

http://en.wikipedia.org/Fibonacci_numbers#In_nature (Last accessed 1/6/14.)

http://en.wikipedia.org/wiki/Golden_ratio (Last accessed 1/6/14.)

http://en.wikipedia.org/wiki/Timaeus(dialogue)#Golden_ratio (Last accessed 1/6/14.)

http://en.wikipedia.org/Vitruvian_man (Last accessed 1/6/14.)

http://selkywolf.com/sweetsong/fairydictionary.html (Last accessed 2/12/14.)

http://www.monstropedia.org (Last accessed 1/3/07.)

http://www.summerlans.com/crossroads/library/dindsenc.htm (Last accessed 10/3/13.)

http://www.symbols.com/encyclopedia/28/281.html (Last accessed 11/4/13.)

http://www.symbols.com/encyclopedia/27/274.html (Last accessed 11/4/13.)

http://www.symbols.com/encyclopedia/14/146.html (Last accessed 11/4/13.)

http://www.symbols.com/encyclopedia/22/225.html (Last accessed 11/4/13.)

http://www.symbols.com/encyclopedia/22/2223.html (Last accessed 11/4/13.)

Index

Alice in Wonderland (film) 68
altered state of consciousness (ASC) 17
anagogical level 163
Apache 32
augury 21
autochthony xxii, xxiv, 3, 7
axis mundi 17
bagua 78
banais rigi 6
Barr, James 163
Basso, Keith 32
Baule 21
biophilia xxiv
Bohm, David 48
Bonewits, Isaac 21
Brenneman, Walter 28
Brosius, J. Peter 31
Buryat 5
Cajete, Gregory 28
Campbell, Joseph 27, 163
Castaneda, Carlos 16, 48
Celts 5, 6
Chatwin, Bruce 35, 111
chi 29
Club des Haschichins 45
cocooning 43
Coleridge, Samuel 112
cohabitants (see appendix)
Congo 4
Congo Square 49
Conjure Dance 49
core shamanism 16
cosmogony 11
cosmogram 62
Cowan, Eliot 7
Daskolos 165
DeChant, Dell 9

Devereux, Paul 45
dindseanchas 28
divination 18
Dolomites 37, 170
Dowson, T. A. 45
Dreamtime 17
ecstasy 16, 67
ecstatic divination 23
Eliade, Mircea 16, 67
entoptic vision 45
Eskimo 5, 7
Euahlayi (Australia) 5
exomatosis 165
feng shui 29, 78
Fibonacci sequence 58
form constants 45
Foxwood, Orion 55, 162
Ghost Dance 49
Golden Mean 58
Goodman, Felicitas 43, 50
Green, Celia 46
Green, Nicholas 97
Grim, John A. 8
Grof, Stanislov 50
Guardians 61, 101
Halifax, Joan 162
Harner, Michael 16, 67
Hemi-sync® 46, 47
Hermetic Principle of Correspondence 21
Higuchi, Tadahiko 30
holon 62
Holotropic® Breathing 50
Huichol 162
humi positio 2
inductive divination 23
Ina Maka 2
initiations 4

instrumental view 8, 14
Jarvik, Murray E. 45
Jaynes, Julian 19
kami 30
Keepers 61, 101
Khakass 5
khalifa Allah 9
Khanty 30, 74
kia 49
Klüver, Heinrich 45
!Kung (Africa) 49
LaBerge, Stephen 47
landnám 29
landschap 97
Law of Association 21
Law of Contagion 21
Law of Similars 21
Lehrman, Frederick 111
Lewis-Williams, J. D. 45
lil' 30
lilenky 30
literal level 163
lithopuncture 62
loric 28
Lower World 17, 68
lung 30
macrobiotics 7
Makers 59, 100
Markides, Kyriacos 165
Mary Poppins (film) 98
Masefield, John 111
Matsubayashi, Kazuo 35
Medicine Wheel 87
metachoric 46
Middle World 17, 70
moral level 163
Nahua 3
Naskapi 18, 22
non-local mind 48
non-ordinary reality 16
num 49
omen, omen text 19
ordinary reality 16
Osho 50
outdooring ceremony 3
Panchamama 2
Penan 31

phi 57
phosphenes 44
place 12
Platonic solids 57
Playtime (film) 14
Pogačnik, Marko 62
Popcorn, Faith 43
pranayama 50
quantum entanglement 22
rewe 68
Robbins, Anthony 50
Sagan, Carl 2
Salwans 37, 170
saman 16
Saorans 69, 74
shaman 16, 67
shamanic state of consciousness (SSC) 17
Shrödinger wave 22
Siegel, Ronald K. 45
sign 154
signifier 155
Smohalla 9
spiritual view 8, 14
songlines 36
sortilege 20
space 11
Stokols, Daniel 8
Talbot, Michael 48
Tara 28
Tati, Jacques 14
Terra Mater 2
terra nullius 113
terra sign (see also Terra Sign index) 113
Tilley, Christopher 97
toponym 31
Trahant, Mark N. 61
tuath 7
Tucker, Mary Evelyn 8
Uisnech, uaisnech 29
Upper World 17, 71
Voodoo 49
Weiner, Eric xviii
West Africa 3
Wilberg, Peter 155
Wovoka 49
yi 30

Terra Signs Index

aa 136, 152
abyssal plain 146
abyssopelagic zone 149
Adriatic Sea 153
Aegean Sea 153
ait 145
Allegheny Highlands 124
alluvial (plain) 126, 127
alluvial fan 127
altiplano 131
Amazon River 118, 119, 122
anastomosing (channel) 118
Andaman Islands 122
Angel Falls 119
Appalachians 135
Arabian Sea 153
arch (desert) 131
arch (coastline) 143
Arches National Monument 131
arctic tundra 129
arcuate (delta) 118
arête 120
arm 141
arroyo 131, 134
ash cone 136
atoll 145
Awjila 134
backshore 140
badlands 151
Badlands National Park 151
Bald Cypress Bayou 117
Baltoro Glacier 121
Barchan (dune) 132
barrier 145
Barringer Crater 154
Bass Harbor 117

batha 123
bathypelagic zone 149
bay 141
bayou 117
beach 140
beck 119
benthic zone 146
Bering Glacier 121
berm 140
Berneray 128
billabong 115, 118
bird's foot (delta) 118
Black Rock Desert 133
Black Sea 153
blanket mire 117
block mountain 135
blowhole 142
Blue Grotto 142
bluff 135
bog 30, 31, 117
Bonneville Salt Flats 133
boreal forest 125
braided (channel) 118
branch 119
brigalow 123
brook 119
Bryce Canyon 150
Bunker Hill 140
burn 119
Buru Rainforest 122
butte 131
caldera 116, 136
Calvin Crater 154
campos 129
canyon 131
cape 141

Cape Cod 142
carr 117
cascade 118
Caspian Sea 153
Castle Rock 138
cataract 118
cave 150
cavern 150
cay 144
Cayman Islands 145
cenote 150
cerrados 129
channel (river) 118
channel (coastline) 143
chaparral 123
chasm 131
Cheddar Gorge 132, 137
Chesapeake Bay Crater 154
Chihuahuan Desert 130
chott 133
cinder cone 136
cirque 120
cliff 135
clitter 138
coastal (plain) 126, 128
coastline 140
Colorado River 118
composite volcano 136
confluence 119
conifers 121
continental shelf 146
continental slope 146
Copper Canyon 132
cove (coastline) 141
cove (valley) 137
crag 138
crater 136
Crater Lake 116
Craters of the Moon 153
creek 119
crevasse 120
cuspate (delta) 118
dale 137
Danakil Depression 137
De La Plata River 119
Dead Sea 153
Death Valley 137

Decaturville Crater 154
deciduous monsoon forest 122
deciduous trees 121, 122
deep sea trench 149
deep water (ocean) 149
dell 137
delta 118, 127
desert 130
Devil's Tower 152
dingle 137
doline 150
dome volcano 136
drumlin 120
dry wash 134
dune (coastline) 140
dune (desert) 132
East Deccan forests 122
Easter Island 145
eddy 118
Ell Pond 117
English Channel 144
epipelagic zone 148
erg 132
escarpment 135
esker 120
estuary 118
eyot 144
fault 115, 135
fen 117
fin 131
firn 120
firth 141, 143
fjord 120, 141
flats 133
floodplain 126 - 128
Florida Everglades 117
Flower Pot Island 143
fold 135
folded mountain 135
foreshore 140
forests 121
fork 119
freshwater 115
fringe 145
Fuji-san 136
fumarole 136, 152
fynbos 123

Ganges River 119
garrigue 123
geyser 152
glacial valley 137
glacier 120
Glacier National Park 126
goblin (wild earth) 149
Goblin Valley State Park 150
gorge 131
graben 115, 135
Grand Canyon 131
Grand Erg Oriental 133
Grand Mesa 131
grassland 126
Great Barrier Reef 146
Great Basin Desert 130
Great Sand Dunes National Park 133
grotto 142
grove 28
gulch 137
gulf 141
Gulf of Mexico 141
gulley, gully 131, 137
guyot 146
gyre 144
hadal zone 149
hamada 132
Hawaiian Islands 145, 153
Hay Tor 138
Haystack Rock 143
headland 141
heathland 123
Hell's Canyon 137
hill 28, 139
hillock 139
Himalayas 135
Hoh Rainforest 125
hollow 137
homogenous (estuary) 118
hoodoo 149
horn 120
horst 135
hot spring 152
Hubbard Glacier 121
ice field 120
iceberg 120
Iguacu Falls 119

impact craters 154
Indian Ocean 153
inlet 141
inselberg 138
intertidal zone 140
island 144
island arc 144
Isle of Palms 141
isthmus 143
Isthmus of Panama 144
Isthmus of Suez 144
Jamaica Pond 117
John Pennekamp Coral Reef State Park 146
jungle 122
kame 120
karst 150
Kata Tjuta 139
Kes Tor 138
kettle hole 116, 117
kettle lake 115, 116
key 144
kill 119
Killary Harbour 121
King's Canyon 137
knob 138
knoll 139
kopje 138
krummholz 135
Kufra 134
kwongan 123
La Pena de Bernal 152
Laacher See 116
lagoon 145
lake 115
Lake Baikal 115, 116
Lake Chad 115, 116
Lake Ronkonkoma 117
Lake Superior 116
Lake Titicaca 116
Land's End 142
lava cave 152
lava flow 152
lava fountain 152
lava plateau 152
lava tube 152
limestone tower 150

Little Rock 138
Llandudno 144
llanos 126, 129
loch 115
lochan 116
Long Island Sound 141
Lostwood Wildlife Refuge 127
lough 115
maar 115, 116
macchia 123
machair 128
machar 128
Malaspina Glacier 121
Mammoth Cave 151
mangal 117
mangrove swamp 117
maquis 123
Marianas Trench 147
marsh 117
matorral 123
Matorral 123
Mauna Loa 136
meandering (channel) 118
Mediterranean Sea 153
mesa 131
mesopelagic zone 148
meteor 154
meteorite 154
microhabitats 122
mire 117
Mississippi River 118, 119, 127
Mojave Desert 130
Molokai 142
monadnock 138
monolith 151
Monument Valley 131
moor 117
moraine 120
Mount Augustus 152
mountain 134
mouth 118
Movile Cave 151
Mt. Monadnock 139
Mt. Ranier 136
Mt. St. Helen 136
Munro 139
muskeg 117

Nag's Head Beach 141
neritic zone 148
ness 141
névé 120
New Jersey Pine Barrens 117
Niagara Falls 119
Niger River 118, 127
Nile River 118, 119
northern coniferous forest 125
oasis 133
oceanic zone 148
Okavango Delta 119
Olduvai Gorge 137
Olympic National Park 125
open sea 144
Osage Hills 127
outcrop 138
outlier 138
overfold 135
oxbow lake 115, 118
pahoehoe 136, 152
pampas 126
Pantanal 118
paramos 126, 129
partially mixed (estuary) 118
passage 143
peatland 117
Peekskill 120
pelagic zone 148
peninsula 141
Persian Gulf 153
phrygana 123
pillow lava 152
pingo 139
pinnacle 149
plain 126
plateau 131
platform 143
Platte River 118
playa 133
polje 150
pond 116
pool 116
pothole 118
prairie 126
prairie pothole 116
promontory 141

Puget Sound 141
puszta 126
puy 136, 139
Rainbow Arch 131
rapids 118
ravine 137
Red Sea 153
reef 145
reg 132
Rhine Valley 137
ridge 138
riffle 119
rift valley 136
rill 119
river 31, 44, 118
river valley 137
rock pool 147
rocky terrain 138
run 119
salt flat 133
salt lake 133
salt pan 133
salt sea 153
salt wedge (estuary) 118
San Francisco Bay 141
Santa Ynes Mountains 123
savanna 129
scarp 135
scrubland 123
sea cave 142
sea cliff 142
sea floor 146
seamounts 146
Seif (dune) 132
Serengeti 130
Seven Hills of Rome 140
Seven Seas 153
shallow water (ocean) 148
shatt 133
sheild volcano 136
Sheyenne National Grasslands 127
shore 140
shott 133
sinkhole 150
skellig 140, 144
skerry 143, 144
slough 117

Sonoran Desert 130
sound 141
source 118
spire 149
spit 141
spring 119, 133
St. Andrew's Beach 141
stack 143
stalactite 150
stalagmite 150
Steamboat Geyser 153
steppe 126, 130
Stone Mountain 152
straight (channel) 118
strait 143
Strait of Gibraltar 144
strandveld 123
strath 137
stream 31, 119
stump 143
Sugarloaf Mountain 139
Suilven 139
swamp 117, 125
tablelands 131
Tafelberg 139
taiga 30, 125
Tall Grass Prairie Preserve 127
tarn 115
temperate deciduous forest 124
temperate evergreen forest 125
temperate rainforest 124
tepui 138
The Black Forest 136
The Needles 143
The Stone Forest 151
thermohaline circulation 144
tidal pool 147
tide pool 147
tombolo 143
tomillares 123
tor 138
trench 146
tributary 119
tropical rainforest 122
tropical scrub 123
tundra 129
Uluru 139

uvala 150
vale 137
valley 137
veldt 126
vents 146
volcano 136
Vosges 136
wadi 134
Walden Pond 117
wash 134
waterfall 118
well 133
wetlands 117
wild earth 149
window 131
woodlands 121
Yangtze River 119
Yellow River 120
Yellowstone National Park 153
Yosemite Falls 119

CPSIA information can be obtained
at www.ICGtesting.com
Printed in the USA
BVHW01s1005200618
R8757300001B/R87573PG519234BVX2B/1/P